RAISING FAITH-FILLED KIDS

RAISING FAITH-FILLED KIDS

Ordinary Opportunities to Nurture Spirituality at Home

TOM McGRATH

LOYOLA PRESS.
A JESUIT MINISTRY
Chicago

LOYOLA PRESS.
A JESUIT MINISTRY

3441 N. Ashland Avenue
Chicago, Illinois 60657
(800) 621-1008
www.loyolapress.com

The Scripture quotations contained herein are from the New Revised Standard Version
Bible: Catholic Edition, copyright © 1993 and 1989 by the Division of Christian
Education of the National Council of the Churches of Christ in the U.S.A.
Used by permission. All rights reserved.

Interior design by Lisa Buckley

Library of Congress Cataloging-in-Publication Data
McGrath, Tom, 1950–
    Raising faith-filled kids : ordinary opportunities to nurture spirituality at
    home / Tom McGrath.
       p. cm.
    ISBN 13: 978-0-8294-1425-7; ISBN 10: 0-8294-1425-8 (pbk.)
    1. Parenting—Religious aspects—Christianity. 2. Child rearing—Religious
    aspects—Christianity. 3. Family—Religious life. 4. Spiritual life—Christianity.
    I. Title.
BV4529 .M384 2000
248.8'45—dc21   00-035408
                                        CIP

Printed in the United States of America
        08 09 10 Versa 10 9 8 7 6

For Marge and Pat McGrath, who, for over fifty years, have faithfully and generously traveled a path of love, with lots of laughs along the way. For Kathleen, Judy, and Patti, my best teachers. And for Tap and Marty and Peggy (and your families); I'm grateful to have companions who bring such joy to the heart.

CONTENTS

Taking action

What you can do now to nurture spiritual life at home

Acknowledgments

There are many people who have contributed directly and indirectly to the development of this book. Even knowing that any list I make will regrettably exclude people who should have been named, still I must express my gratitude specifically to:

Betty Schmidt, George Cihocki, Fathers Bill O'Mara and William Henkel, John Fahey, David Ives, Joan Finnegan, Robert E. Burns, Kevin Axe, Dick Frisbie, Catherine Johns and Frank Tisinski, Bill Burns, Greg Pierce, Bonnie Bachman, Dan Grippo, Linus Mundy, Neal and Pat Kluepfel, Michael Leach, Father John Smyth, Frank and Eileen Gaughan, Maureen Abood, and Jonna Mogab, who, at significant times along the way, have encouraged my writing.

My coworkers at Claretian Publications, who provide the most creative and enjoyable community imaginable, including Catherine O'Connell-Cahill, my partner in writing *At Home with Our Faith,* for her incredible talent, unerring insights, and depth of character; and, especially, Tom Wright, Patrice Tuohy, Meinrad Scherer-Emunds, Dianne Walde, Mary Lynn Hendrickson, Carmen Aguinaco, Anne Marie O'Kelley, Joel Schorn, Fran Hurst, Heidi Schlumpf, Kevin

Clarke, John Kuenster, Anita Jackson, and Maria Hickey for their specific and highly professional help in pulling together the material for this manuscript. And to Father Mark Brummel, C.M.F., and the Claretians of the Eastern Province, who respect and support the spiritual roles of the laity.

Polly Berrien Berends, Dolores Curran, Kathleen O'Connell-Chesto, John Shea, and Richard Rohr, O.F.M., whose work has opened my eyes to see that being a parent is a spiritual path.

Father Bob Bolser, C.S.V., and the clerics of St. Viator Parish in Chicago, who nurture my family's faith day by day. Bernie and Rosie Tholl, Jeannie and Jerry Pitzen, Regina and Jim King, Dorothy Gorski, Betty Stuckey, Erroll and Kathy Ortiz, Jane Vertucci, Chris Gucwa, and Mary Ellen Matheson, our faith-sharing group, who long ago, on a weekly basis, revealed that God did, indeed, live in our home. And to Dave and Patti Melzer, and now Heather and Gerard Baum, who open their home and hearts to our parish's teens.

Kevin Shanley and Phil Kennedy, who have been steadfast friends and, along with the Monday Night Priory Group, have been fellow explorers of the spirituality of imperfection. For Joe Shanley, Phil Twomey, and John Rohan, with whom I discovered life more abundantly at SSCA in 1967.

The book club group: Bob Hamilton and Keiren O'Kelly, Peter Graff and Ann O'Hara Graff, Colleen and Bill Burns, who taught us it's more fun to struggle with the art of parenting together than on our own.

My parents and siblings and their spouses and children, who make it easy to believe in a loving God.

My daughters Judy and Patti, and especially my wife Kathleen, who supported me despite long weekends and evenings spent grumbling at the computer, and accompanied me through that murky time when all seems lost and all that's left to us is to be carried along by the faith and goodness of those who love us.

I came that they may have life,
and have it abundantly.

JESUS CHRIST (JOHN 10:10)

CHAPTER ONE

Good News for Parents

You Can Pass On a Living Faith

I was at my friend Tina's house for a barbecue recently. Tina is a wonderful woman, a great mother, kind to her friends and generous to strangers. Her home is bright and welcoming. She prays daily and does what she can to maintain conscious contact with God throughout the day.

Tina heard I was working on a book. "What's it about?" she asked brightly.

"It's about how parents can raise kids with a living faith in God," I replied.

Tina's face fell, looking sad and guilty. "Oh, that's something I'm just no good at. I really need a book like that."

Tina, I'm writing this book with you in mind. Because, you see, you *are* good at raising your kids with a living faith— the faith you have surrounds them as they grow. Beyond that, you have everything it takes to do the job well. And finally, many parents I meet feel, as you do, that they are totally inept when it comes to raising their kids with faith, so they don't recognize the natural steps they can take to nurture their family's experience of faith right in their homes.

3

I find that many normally competent people appear to be lost at sea regarding this important aspect of their children's lives. They feel guilty for not being more intentional or active in nurturing their children's faith, yet they seem unsure about how to remedy the situation. It's as if they're being asked to do something they haven't had the least experience with—like teaching their kids to speak Gaelic, Urdu, or Swahili.

Yet by and large, the parents I talk to attempt to live a spiritually grounded life. Maybe they don't go to church as often as they feel they should or pray as much as they wish they did. But they have faith in God, pray regularly, and live in ways that express and deepen their relationship with their creator. They are not faithless people. If pushed on the topic, most would say that faith has been extremely valuable to them. In fact, what most pains them is that they fear they will be unable to pass along the benefits of this faith to the children they love so dearly.

But we need to understand how faith operates. You don't pass on a living faith like a quarterback handing off a football to a running back. And parents don't create faith. Faith comes from God, and God has placed the seed of faith in each child. It's a longing for connection to deep and profound truth that is planted within each one of them. Parents have a major influential role in how prepared the child is and how well the faith is nurtured. But we don't create faith, possess faith, or control it. Faith is a relationship like the relationship between a vine and its branches. Faith flows. *Our main task is to encourage the flow and not block it.*

Many parents underestimate their ability to influence their children's faith development. I think that's because they underestimate the value of ordinary family life as a channel of faith. And they also underestimate the power of their own faith—no bigger than a mustard seed, they worry—to influence their children's faith development.

I hope, through this book, to help you see with new eyes, to enable you to look at the activities and interactions of daily living in your family and see in them sacramental moments that point to a loving God. This book is not going to ask you to disrupt your daily routines, but rather to see those moments within the give-and-take of daily living as ways in which God is present and calling you to live life more abundantly.

FINDING THE TREASURE WE ALREADY HAVE

Many people fear that if they answer the call to become more spiritually alive they will be required to make radical changes in their living situation. The fantasy they fear possibly takes the shape of having to leave their family, move to a remote mission in a destitute country, and live on wild honey and locusts. Becoming more spiritually alive does involve radical changes. But I have found that rather than taking precious things away from me, the changes open my eyes to new depths and riches that are all around me. Rather than losing something, I gain everything.

Perhaps you've seen the program on public television, "Antiques Roadshow," where people bring old treasures and oddities they find or have stored in their homes, attics, or garages and get them appraised by experts. It's great fun to see what people own and to learn how much the items turn out to be worth. Some of the pieces are worth no more than whatever sentimental value they hold; other items are worth a fortune.

My favorite viewing moment came when a nice lady brought in a painting of the signing of the Declaration of Independence. As it happens, this patriotic painting was

5

worth no more than fifty dollars. But while she was standing in line waiting her turn for the appraisal, she decided to clean the frame. When she removed the frame, one of the expert appraisers caught sight of something amazing and unexpected. It turns out that a later, and less talented, artist used the back of an existing painting to paint Washington, Jefferson, Hancock, and Co. But the original painting—kept in pristine condition within the frame all these years—was a rare and wonderful painting by a colonial-era painter. It was worth hundreds of thousands of dollars.

All this time the people in that home had a treasure within reach and never knew it. We all do. It may not be worth cold, hard currency. But in fact the treasure we are heirs to is much more valuable. Because what is more valuable than life? And what Jesus promises us—whether in cloister, mission, monastery, or messy, chaotic home—is to give us life more abundantly. We just have to have eyes to see.

In this book I will talk about ideas to help nurture your children's faith that can be applied in family living. But I'll also spend three chapters talking about your spiritual life. The truth is that being a parent is indeed a spiritual path. This is your mission, should you choose to accept it.

We are not doing this job alone. In nurturing faith in our kids, we have at our disposal the power of our own spiritual tradition. Committing to a spiritual path affords us disciplines, practices, and the example of holy heroes and companions to accompany us on our way. We have the example and support of other parents who take this duty seriously. And we have the Holy Spirit, whom Jesus promised, to serve as our guide. The first steps in getting started are to acknowledge our intention to raise our children well, ask God for help, and respond when the next ordinary opportunity arises.

MAKING CONNECTIONS IN A WORLD
CUT ADRIFT

Odds are that if you picked up this book, you care deeply about your child and you want your child to know the benefits of having a strong and living faith. That's a perfect and wonderful place to start. Realize that God has called you to this moment and will provide the ways and means to lead you where you need to go next.

Modern life often works to disconnect us from sources of strength, health, healing, and support. It's time to re-connect. Start where you are, find spiritual companions, and ask God to lead you.

A quick and impression-istic look at the current envi-ronment in which parents operate puts our situation in context. The age we live in is not conducive to passing our faith on to our children. Many of the social supports for reli-gion have been left by the wayside, while self-reliance and individualism have almost become religions in themselves. When our immigrant ances-tors came to this country, religious customs and the local church formed a life raft in their new and turbulent world. Religious customs in the home and neighborhood conveyed a definite identity and served to pass along values and norms. The local church was often the center of the social and political life of the community as well as a very visible center of religious and spiritual activity. The local parish or commu-nity church afforded a worldview that in turn provided co-

> *The experience we seek lies within our own heart. Once we are grounded in our own inner love all we need to know will be revealed to us.*
>
> Anne Johnson and Vic Goodman, *The Essence of Parenting: Becoming the Parent You Want to Be*

herence and meaning to people building new lives in a new and sometimes hostile culture. The church provided identity and meaning; it was an anchor in people's lives in those days, one that many people have seen fit to let drift away. More and more, though, people are recognizing that the culture, though seductive in appearance, can be shallow and hostile, and they are looking for that anchor once again.

The focus and pace of our world also work against faith development in our kids. So much of the world's focus is on the external and transitory. Think of all the commercial messages your kids face each day. Every one of these messages lures us to concentrate on the immediate gratification of some temporary (and usually artificial) need. The gratification is short-lived or even nonexistent. This rapid cycle of raised, then dashed, hopes breeds cynicism in our kids. It's hard to have faith when your credibility has been toyed with since you were old enough to watch your first commercial for a breakfast cereal or a superhero action figure ("some pieces sold separately"). Our kids need just as much exposure to messages that inspire faith and promote lasting values.

Modern life, for many families, is overscheduled, scattered, and frantic. Many families find little opportunity to pursue regular practice of religion and faith. And because so many families move frequently, many children grow up without regular connection with grandparents (who traditionally play an important role in training children in the practice of the faith) or a faith community where they know people and are known.

DEVELOPING FAITH IN A COMMERCIAL, CYNICAL CULTURE

Our world looks with suspicion at faith in God yet blindly

accepts advertising claims that a new kind of toilet-bowl cleaner will make life more exciting and fulfilling. This double standard breeds cynicism in our children, and a kind of hopelessness that manifests itself in the reluctance to commit to any person, institution, or tradition of belief. Our children are hungry for good things to eat, and we're handing them junk food.

Too often, religious experience or spirituality is presented as yet another consumer good: something to acquire, possess, or control by taking ownership of. And so we dabble in yoga, see what New Age has to offer, even dig out that old rosary for a couple of days. We dip a toe into the spiritual pool, but we never leave the shallow end. When people treat spirituality and religion as products or wonder drugs offering fast-acting relief, their experience will be empty and illusory.

Yet it doesn't have to be this way. We are not hopeless and helpless. We can raise our children with a living faith by inviting them to join us on a spiritual path. We don't need degrees in theology to introduce our children to the principles and practices that can make their lives deeper, more meaningful, and more fulfilling. If you want your children to grow up in an atmosphere of faith, introduce faith as a natural and regular part of your relationship with them.

Family life presents ordinary opportunities to nurture children's faith, to introduce them to such building-block concepts as trust, respect, belief, service, love, and reliance on a higher power. There are steps you can take, practices to engage in as a family and with each of your children individually. There are attitudes to foster and experiences to encourage. Through exposure to your own faith and the interactions you have with your children that are illuminated by your faith, you can invite them to begin a lifelong journey of discovery that tells them who they are and why they are here. Are there any lessons in life more important than these?

USING WHAT WE'RE ALREADY DOING

When I look back at my own religious upbringing, I see that I was immersed in a whole culture that was steeped in Catholicism as it was experienced in that era (late fifties through early seventies). It was quite a cast of characters that surrounded us. The nuns and dedicated laypeople who taught us at school; the pastor and priests who celebrated Mass, administered the sacraments, and tended to our souls; neighbors who were also strong believers; extended family members who were as likely to talk about religious practice or beliefs as they were about the White Sox or the latest political scandal; and my parents—all played a role in conveying not only the content of the faith but also a worldview that showed that faith was a valued element in living a full and worthy life.

Yet as I look back on all those activities established to teach me about my religion, it was the ordinary human interactions of daily life that had the most profound effect on my future faith. It was the painting of Jesus that hung over our sofa; it was saying grace before every meal, helping the men of the parish set up the chairs for the annual spaghetti dinner, or helping Mom make decorations for the Altar and Rosary Society's fashion show. All these had the most impact on my developing faith. It was the way my parents would never dream of pocketing the proceeds when given too much change at a store or the way we were gently but firmly corrected when we used rude language about people of other backgrounds or races.

One of my strongest memories of growing in the faith occurred on a snowy day in December. My dad was teaching religious education to eighth-grade boys. I was probably in fourth or fifth grade. They were a tough bunch, but Dad liked their spunk. During the past month, they had collected canned goods, toys, and clothing for newly arrived immigrants. It may have been the first time in years these adolescents had thought of someone other than themselves. Such is life at that age. Dad brought me along to help the group deliver the gifts. As we drove, snow began to fall in thick, heavy flakes.

I was nervous and embarrassed about meeting the recipients of our largesse. I thought they might be embarrassed or uncomfortable. We didn't know their language, and I wasn't sure they understood ours. But Dad was effusive, vocal, and eager to meet these newly arrived neighbors. His warmth won the day. People welcomed us into their homes—sparsely furnished, spare apartments. I remember one home in particular. We stood in the kitchen talking to a proud man and his very shy wife. She sat at the kitchen table on one of two chairs, her head down modestly, but a smile crept to her face as the men struggled to communicate across languages and cultures. The room was bare except for a beautiful silver crucifix, the obvious centerpiece of their home.

The snow continued to fall, transforming the city into a pristine and hopeful world. The day even seemed to transform those eighth-graders, who now were wide-eyed as little children, their guard down, their innocence restored.

We made a number of stops, and I eventually got chilled while carting the food up open back stairways and down windy gangways. When we arrived home, I realized for perhaps the first time what a blessing central heating is. Mom was cooking dinner, and I've never smelled anything more wonderful. Mom welcomed us with hugs and encouragement to change into warm, dry clothes.

I sat on the sofa with my brother, Pat, and we watched *A Christmas Carol*—the real one with Alastair Sim as Scrooge. I felt at home in a whole new way. We had been part of life—giving gifts and receiving them, connecting with others, some of them in real need. We blessed them and they blessed us,

God's love circulating freely all around. I looked out our front window, and in the light of the streetlamp, I saw the snow tumbling down, like grace, as far as the eye could see.

Living faith is not something you impose on your children; it's something that informs the day-to-day moments you live together as a family. It's not something you can box up and hand to them. There is no formula or prescribed set of actions that will do the trick. There is just living and loving together and taking opportunities to share what you have found to be of great value—your beliefs and practices of living in God's love.

Robert Wuthnow said in *Growing Up Religious:*

> Effective religious socialization comes about through embedded practices; that is, through specific, deliberate religious activities that are firmly intertwined with the daily habits of family routines, of eating and sleeping, of having conversations, of adorning the spaces in which people live, of celebrating the holidays, and of being part of a community. Compared with these practices, the formal teachings of religious leaders often pale in significance.

In short, kids get faith by living in a home where faith also dwells.

Children don't arrive equipped with instruction manuals, and they certainly don't come with guarantees. To be a parent is to enter into a relationship of grace and mystery and wonder. About the only guarantee we can expect in such circumstances is that our God, who is a loving God, will meet us in the midst of that relationship, eager to bring us all to abundant life. Working on faith means building up relationships—with God, self, and others.

Relationships, especially the relationship between parent

and child, are always more art than science. And usually, coming armed with clinical formulas is not the best way to approach a relationship. That's like trying to master the tango just by reading a book. The book may help you get the general idea and inspire you to try, but it's no substitute for getting out on the dance floor with a partner in your arms and, for style, a rose in your teeth.

Faith is a relationship of love with our God, played out across the days of our lives. It's supported by the disciplines and practices of the Christian tradition that we make our own. So to raise your kids with a living faith, you must first be immersed in a living faith. This doesn't mean you have to be perfect. It only means that you are in relationship with God. The reality of that primary relationship will filter into all your relationships. When you love God, you will naturally bring that love into the care and feeding of your children. "For those who do not love a brother or sister whom they have seen, cannot love God whom they have not seen." Do we really want to take a chance on that love? And are we willing to use the ups and downs of family life to awaken that love within us?

It takes practice to see the "moreness" of life. For example, in front of me as I write is an old teacup. It is chipped and the colors are out of date—very seventies—and I suppose it should be easy to just toss it out. But my father-in-law used that cup for years before he died. He drank his iced coffee from it. When I look at it, I remember years ago, sipping hot tea from it with one or the other of my daughters on my lap, reading the comics together on Saturday mornings. And when I used the cup, back then as now, it would be a silent prayer to my father-in-law, the grandfather who died before he could meet his lovely granddaughters, to help me be a good husband to his daughter and a good father to his granddaughters. That teacup spoke to me then, as it speaks to me now, of grace and the sacredness of ordinary things. Family life *is* religious life.

CATCHING THE ACTION RIGHT WHERE IT IS

Families are in a unique position to pass on the faith. "A Family Perspective in Church and Society," a document of the Committee on Marriage and Family Life of the National Conference of Catholic Bishops, says, "Family constitutes a special revelation and realization of ecclesial communion, and for this reason too, [the family] can and should be called the domestic church." The bishops added, "The family is not merely *like* the Church, but is truly Church." This is not to say that families ought to be churchy, but in the normal course and messiness of daily life, they do what the church was commissioned by Jesus to do: be the body of Christ in the world.

The saddest thing I can imagine is to arrive at the empty-nest time of life, look back, and echo these words of Jacob: "Surely the Lord is in this place and I did not know it!" I believe that God is revealed to us through the ordinary events in family life. You don't have to become someone you're not in order to experience this revelation. You just have to pay attention to the subtle ways God operates in the life of your family. Perhaps you can begin this book with the prayer "O God, open my eyes so that I may see."

In this book I offer only my own experience, strength, and hope. I don't pretend it is a final or definitive answer to the questions raised. Rather, I hope it helps you wrestle with the questions and discover your own wisdom. Take what you like, and leave the rest.

Most of my examples will come from the Catholic tradition. That's the tradition I follow on my own spiritual path. It's a rich tradition and in some ways is very family friendly.

One of the best things about Catholicism is that it sees all of life as sacramental—as capable of transmitting God's grace. That means every object in your home, every relationship, every moment of family life is capable of revealing your connection with God. But many spiritual paths lead toward the same goal. If you come from a different religious tradition, I'm certain that many of the principles set forth here can be adapted easily to make sense in your world as well.

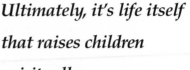

Ultimately, it's life itself that raises children spiritually.

Polly Berrien Berends

My hope in this book is to help you see more clearly in the mundane details of your daily family life moments of grace, the availability of God's presence, and the wonder that we are all held in the palm of God's hand. In the seeing, you will point to that reality for your child to see as well. And you will raise your child surrounded by a living faith.

*Human life is the
operating system on which
all God's programs run.*

ARCHBISHOP

DANIEL E. PILARCZYK

CHAPTER TWO

The Basic Question

What Do You Wish for This Child?

Do you remember holding your child when he or she was just days and weeks old? I imagine it's a most vivid memory. The miracle of birth gave way to the unfolding of a life. Oh, God, how your heart was full to overflowing in those first days of the child's new life, looking down at the brand-new, never-to-be-duplicated person-in-progress so small in your hands.

The opening words of the Catholic rite of baptism are addressed to parents and godparents as they are in that mood of heightened anticipation. "What do you wish for this child?" It's a good question. The simple answer parents and godparents give that day is, "Baptism." But that's a loaded statement. We each pack a lot of our own hopes and fears, dreams and worries into that wish.

Kathleen and I were expecting our first daughter, Judy, when we moved into a house in our current parish. We had moved in too late to join the regularly scheduled baptism-preparation class, but Brother Bill Haesaert, C.S.V., kindly offered to come to our house and review the material with us.

We sat amid the boxes in our new living room, responding to that question, "What do you wish for this child?" We looked at that question from several viewpoints.

- That of the parents
- That of the parish community that welcomed this child
- That of our larger family, which would join us on the day of the baptism ceremony
- That of the church as a whole, a universal church whose mission it is to bring forth the reign of God

"What do you wish for this child?" Brother Bill asked us. Through the give-and-take of our exploration, it became clear to me that I had a number of wishes for my child, many of them seemingly contradictory. I wanted our soon-to-be-born child to have a life of adventure and great meaning, yet I didn't want her to suffer undue upset. I wanted her to have a life of great fulfillment but little pain. I wanted her to know the Lord as her shepherd without having to travel through the valley of darkness. In short, I wanted the resurrection without the cross.

A parent's first desire, of course, will be the safety of this child. It's our deep human instinct to care for this defenseless infant. Within parents is a fierce protective impulse. I'm sure I'm not the only dad who stood in the darkness a long time beside his sleeping child in the first days of her life, vowing to protect her from any and all harm that might come her way.

Yet even as we make that vow, we know we will not be able to keep it. We know all too well how life can be harsh, cruel, hurtful. For all its beauty, the world has also shown us its ugliness. For all its joys, it's given us bitter tears of sorrow and pain.

If we want our children truly to live life to its fullest, we know that our wish contains the admission of pain, difficulty, disappointment, and sorrow. So we cannot wish half a life for them—the plastic existence that stays on the surface and never feels pain because it doesn't feel joy either. Such a life feels nothing.

Many parents say, "I want the best for my children." What constitutes "the best"? If my children cannot avoid pain—and clearly that is not possible in this mortal life—then my hope is that they will know a God who can meet them in their joys and in their sorrows, accompany them with strength in their exultation and in their pain, and offer them life on a new level that transcends all pain and sorrow.

I want them to meet the One who offers living water to quench their deepest thirst. I want them to spend their days tasting the Bread of Life. These images may seem fanciful or merely poetic. The fact is that these images of Jesus are among our best attempts to describe a new reality—the reality we come to know through a life of faith. I want my children to know that reality.

If the choice is to live shallowly to avoid the pain (perhaps to gain the whole world but lose their souls) or to live fully and accept the pain, I want something for my children that makes sense of the pain. They need to learn an approach to life that offers them a fullness of living that more than makes sense of life's pain and disappointments (after all, sometimes they don't make sense). I believe that a life of faith enables us to go through and even transcend the pain and disappointment. Our tradition tells us that Jesus is the way, the truth, and the life. This phrase is either a glib cliché or a most profound mystery worthy of a lifelong commitment.

INVITE THE MYSTERY

We approach the dark side of the mystery when we bring our child to the waters of baptism. Whether we bring a defenseless infant in our arms, a toddler holding tightly to our hand, or a teenager striding forward to the baptismal font under his own steam, each child is vulnerable in this life. In the sacrament of baptism we enact that danger. Those to be baptized are plunged into the waters, and they die with Jesus. This action speaks to our fear. But we also enact the second movement of the drama. We place on the ones baptized a glistening white garment, and we hand them a candle, the light of Christ. Thus, they rise with Jesus as well, bearing a light that cannot be extinguished. This is our hope and our faith.

To raise a child with a living faith is not a pious, shallow affair. It means tackling life's deepest, most troubling question head-on, in order to find an answer that you can reliably pin your hopes on. This is not an answer such as the solution to an algebraic equation. It's not a formula you can write down or look up in a book when you need it. Rather, it's a way of living that leads to a deepening understanding of this truth over time. It's a way of grace. It's the answer to your deepest desire, the one you felt the day you first held your child in your hands. And to raise your child with a living faith, you must live the faith with your child. "How do you get to Carnegie Hall?" goes the old joke. The answer is, was, and always will be, "Practice, practice, practice."

KNOW YOUR OWN MOTIVES

It's good to examine the hopes and expectations we have for our children. The wish that our children will have a good relationship with God can be a mixed bag too. A good follow-up question to "What do you wish for this child?" would be "Why?" Not all answers are equal. Few, if any, of us have totally pure motives. It's possible to want the right thing for some wrong reasons.

For example, some parents want their children to "get religion" as a strategy of repression, a way of keeping them "good kids" who are too constrained to stray from the prescribed path. These are the parents who send their kids to religious schools, not for true spiritual formation, but to "keep them in line." That's coercion, an abuse of religion, and to the extent that it impedes the child's full human development, it's an abuse of the child. With all the dangerous choices facing children (drugs, gangs, guns, premature sexual intimacy, and so forth), it's tempting to want to put religion on them like a harness to keep them on the straight and narrow. But when it's imposed rather than chosen, that harness becomes a straitjacket.

Some parents want religion for their children as a way of placating God. It's often not looked at this baldly, but hidden within this wish is a belief that if my kid is outwardly religious, God will be kept happy, and a happy God won't let my child know any earthly harm. This is superstition, the belief that through our actions we can control God.

Because becoming a parent is an awesome prospect, I felt both those temptations the days we brought our two daughters to the altar for baptism. I thought of the forlorn and dismal teenagers I saw hanging out at the park, with their antisocial T-shirts and eerie, empty eyes, the malt liquor cans strewn about their feet, and my wish was that somehow religion would magically steer my daughters from encountering the demons that led those kids to those park benches. But there are demons in all of us, and if we don't face them, we'll never become fully alive.

On the days of my daughters' baptisms, I also wanted to bribe God. I wanted to offer anything I could scrounge up to protect these precious angels from accident and illness, from tragedy and trauma. I suppose my unspoken, childish hope went something like "See, God. We're all jumping through these hoops for you. Now, I hope you remember that when you're handing out the cancer and the car accidents and the avalanches and the tragic shooting of the innocent bystander." This is shallow faith. It's also an insult to God, reducing God to a scorekeeper who is on the take.

As we hold this precious life in our hands, a life we can love more than our very own, it's understandable that we would try to muster all available clout and play all the angles for this child. But at our depths as humans we hold a more profound wish: that our child will know God truly and deeply in this world and be sustained through all of life with that love.

BEWARE OF WHAT YOU ASK FOR

We want our children to know God truly and deeply. This can be a dangerous wish. The big critique of religion is that it's the opiate of the masses, a way of taming people's true spirits, a way of keeping us docile and malleable. And as long as religion gets enacted in our lives out of fear and superstition, that critique is valid. But true faith is radical and freeing. Authentic faith provides no straitjackets, no promises of protection from mortal harm. And certainly it's not tame. Think of St. Francis of Assisi, who was eagerly following his father's script for living "the good life" when faith took root. The next thing you know, he was standing buck naked in the town square, relinquishing all his father's possessions (including the clothes he'd just removed) as well as the plans his father had laid out for his prosperous future.

Faith can prompt your college-graduate daughter to become a lay missionary in a war-torn country rather than pursue that scholarship to dental school. Real religion can lead your sixth-grade son to befriend the outcast at school, letting go of his grip on popularity and the easiness of being in the "in crowd." Faith will even lead our kids to question our values and behaviors (ouch!) and to challenge us to examine our own lives and choices.

You can see why parents might be reluctant for their kids to take this religion thing too seriously. Staying well behaved and doing what's expected is fine. Going off to follow God, well, that's another thing altogether!

Christianity is about seeing. It's not about earning or achieving. It's about relationship rather than results or requirements.

Richard Rohr, O.F.M.

Living out one's faith is not a path to safety—except the ultimate and only safety we can know, the constant and all-encompassing love of God. Neither is it a path to protection—except the ultimate protection of being in the hands of God. But it is the path to which all of us are called. Most of us won't become Francis of Assisis or Joan of Arcs or Dorothy Days or Anne Franks. But faith can be as real to us and to our children as it was to these saints who have gone before us. That's the kind of faith worth having.

This book is for parents who want their children to have the benefit of faith to sustain them through their lives. It's for those who have come to believe that faith and a spiritual life are treasures to be shared and that a life without a deeper spiritual meaning is empty, a life not fully lived.

As Jesus presented it, having religious faith is not bowing down to "the Big Guy Upstairs." Rather, real faith recognizes and seeks union with the God who dwells among us,

Taking action 1

How to make your desires for your child more real

Stop a moment to ask yourself, "What do I wish for my child?" Try to put your thoughts into words. Think back to when your child first arrived in your life—how you felt, what your hopes were. Think of difficult times your child has faced—anything from a life-threatening illness to a difficult time at school. Were you able to deepen your understanding of your hopes for this child? Did you find that these hopes helped you choose a course of action to help your child? Do your actions now support the likely fulfillment of these hopes in your child's life?

Recognize that your wishes for your child may be mixed. This is only human. For example, you might wish that your child will be someone who stands up for the underdog, but you don't want your child embroiled in conflict. Remember, our wishes are not a blueprint for our children; they're a guide and an impetus to *us* in how

we raise them. Acknowledging our mixed wishes will only make it easier to understand what impulses are at work in us as we try to raise our children with faith.

Keep your eye on the prize. It's easy for parents to get caught up in the day-to-day concerns of raising a family and lose sight of the magnitude of this adventure. It pays to find ways to frequently remember your deepest wishes. As Sister Catherine Bertrand, S.S.N.D., said about keeping her religious vocation fresh and vibrant, "I need to remember the desires of my younger days."

Use birthdays as an occasion to write (or ponder) your thoughts and feelings for this child. It's a time to do a sort of check-in with yourself on how you feel you're doing as you try to launch this child well into life. What have been the year's ups and downs?

What new qualities and strengths do you see in your child? What are the challenges on his or her plate these days? Comment on the child's spiritual growth.

Celebrate

your child's baptismal anniversary. That night prepare a special meal and light the child's baptismal candle (if you still have it around) or another candle that you keep for special occasions with this child. For grace, say a prayer thanking God for the special gifts of this child. Maybe each person at the table can say one thing he or she admires or appreciates about the honoree. You can also be mindful of name days (the feast day of the saint your child is named after) to reinforce those baptismal wishes.

Find a symbol of the

wishes brought to that baptism day and give it to your child. It might be a cross, a rosary owned by a grandparent or other ancestor, a Bible, or some other religious item or image that conveys the yearnings you have for your child's spiritual growth. This symbol can become part of your child's life day in and day out, a steady presence that reminds you both that there is a deeper purpose to your lives than you normally see and that it has its place within your family.

Invite the child's

godparents to put their wishes into words in a letter for the child. Save it and share it at a time the child is ready to understand it. For many families, the role of godparent can be simply honorary, but it ought to be more than that. Kids need significant adults, connected to the family, who also stand for and try to enact the values the family espouses. Most of the time these lessons will be unspoken. It's the godparent's life that will speak volumes. But it wouldn't hurt to make this influence more explicit on occasion.

Here's a letter I wrote for one of my godsons on the day of his baptism. His parents are holding it for him until he's old enough to begin to understand it. The letter accompanied a Celtic cross made of peat, turf from the fields of Ireland.

Dear Brian Thomas,

I chose this gift especially for you because it symbolizes so much of what's important about your christening day.

The cross is the central symbol of the faith we welcome you into today. It's the symbol of the faith shared by your parents and grandparents, aunts and uncles, cousins and sisters. It's the same sign we will all trace on your forehead, the sign we will make as we gather together at church today. It's the same sign that we make before we eat our meals and even, by some, in the batter's box or at the free throw line. This sign reveals a great truth about life: If we die to ourselves, we can rise to new life. It means that even when all seems hopeless, we still are not lost. There is a good shepherd who is searching us out no matter how far we stray.

On this particular cross are images from stories that show God created us, loves us, cares about our welfare, and acts in human history. Our story of faith reveals that God loves us so much he sent us a child, a precious son like you, Brian, to grow in wisdom, age, and grace and to dwell among us and show us the way to eternal life.

The cross itself is formed from the very turf of Ireland, the soil of your ancestors. On this land they lived and struggled, rejoiced, loved, hungered, and died. On this island lived poets and playwrights, warriors and fools, saints cherished for heroic acts of charity and thugs feared for their acts of festering resentment. The land can be gentle, soft, and nurturing or some of the world's most barren and cruel. Our roots go deep into that soil; our souls are fed by deep springs in that land.

Brian Thomas, these symbols are particular to the Catholic faith and to the Irish soil. But they go beyond that too. They are universal symbols: Love your neighbor and love the earth you and your neighbors must share. You are born into a world that offers tremendous promise and tremendous challenge. I pray that this cross will be an anchor for you, holding you firm to the values that are your birthright and inheritance. I pray that the truths it points to will be a compass for you and guide you on the path to peace.

Welcome to the story, our common story of life and faith.

Your godfather,
Uncle Tom

the one who sits at our kitchen table, walks our halls, and is as close to us as our very heartbeat.

Our greatest fears and greatest hopes mingle in the waters of baptism. We bring our child to the waters, confident that God's ways will lead this child on good paths. Although the ways of God are beyond our understanding, in the long run they make better sense and speak to our deepest longings better than anything else we can find. As Peter said to Jesus, "Lord, to whom can we go? You have the words to eternal life."

When all is said and done,
I consider my family both my
blessing and my best work.

JOHN LITHGOW

CHAPTER THREE

A "Family" Business
The Commitment We Owe Our Kids

Years ago, when they installed the first computer system at our workplace, we'd turn on our machines in the morning and this question would pop up on all the computer screens: "What job will you do?" Of course, the point of the question was to prompt us to click on one of the menu items listed below. But I always thought it was a good meditation moment. Before getting into the mundane details of the day's routine, you had a chance to tackle one of life's big questions. "What job will I do? Why am I here? What's my purpose?" My computer asked the question of that famed philosopher who wrote, "What's it all about, Alfie?"

I urge all parents to ask that question too. A story may help explain how my wife and I related this question to being parents. Kathleen and I came to an important discovery early on in our stint as Mom and Dad. The day after Judy was born, it dawned on us that as the mother and father of this helpless little infant we were now on duty twenty-four hours a day, seven days a week, for the next eighteen to twenty-one years—for the rest of our lives, actually. The very thought was

29

overwhelming. We wondered, "How will we ever do it? We're not up to it!"

Since then I've heard other young parents ask the same question. Some friends who are just starting their families have confided their absolute terror at the thought of having thrust upon them the awesome task of being totally responsible for another's care, feeding, growth, and well-being. I remember one young woman with a two-week-old asking in bewilderment, "Like, when do you get some time off?" My best advice was, "Whenever they sleep, you sleep." Having a child is one of the most life-altering experiences you will ever face. And usually the magnitude of the change to your life comes somewhat as a surprise.

In discussing our own fears of how to respond to the challenges of parenthood, Kathleen and I hit upon an idea, a mental and moral framework that helped us. When we were first married, we toyed—as young dreamers do—with the idea of owning our own business. I'd always wanted to own a real Chicago-style hot-dog stand. My first job was peeling potatoes at just such a place when I was a kid on Chicago's South Side. As we talked about such a start-up, we realized that building a business wouldn't be a lark; it would take a tremendous commitment. We'd have to be there day and evening, rain or shine. We'd have to work weekends and some holidays, without any sick days. It would take work and luck, but over time we could enjoy results that were truly worthwhile. Our efforts and sacrifices would be worth it to build our family business.

We never did buy that hot-dog stand, but we began to think of parenthood in the same light. Raising children according to our best hopes wasn't just a lark; it would take a tremendous commitment. We'd be on duty day and evening (and the middle of the night!), rain or shine. We'd have to work weekends, all holidays, with no days off when we were under the weather. It would take work and luck, but over time, we hoped, we would come to enjoy results that were truly worthwhile. Raising our daughters would be our family business.

Making that top-priority decision has made all the subsequent decisions easier. It wasn't as if every time we had to change a diaper or drive one of our girls to the library we faced a major trauma. It was simply that moment's contribution to the family business of raising our daughters well. All of the countless, sometimes minor, decisions we made on a daily basis flowed from our overarching decision to raise our daughters as well as we knew how. This commitment applied to holding the line on bedtimes or the need for them to pick up their toys; giving them their medicine; not letting them watch certain TV shows that, though popular, we didn't approve of; or simply redirecting their attention to something fun instead of constantly saying, "Don't!" when they were intent on playing with the gas burners. After that initial commitment to our daughters was made, all the other decisions and efforts were just additional contributions to the family business.

ARE YOU LOOKING FOR SHORTCUTS?

There's no quickie recipe for raising spiritually grounded kids. Marva J. Dawn wrote in the April 1999 issue of *Theology Today:*

> We who treasure children and want to nurture faith
> and faith-life in them would often rather have a quick
> and easy miracle than the endless, frequently burden-
> some discipline (for ourselves and them) of genuine
> Christian training. But the long months of . . . be-
> ing extraordinarily careful and watchful and patient

and diligent, of additional practices and ardent prayer, of resisting temptations and maintaining persistent self-control, of loving labor and sensitive safekeeping are not only necessities for the spiritual formation of the children; these nurturing disciplines on our part are also worth the efforts for our own sake.

Lest my portrayal of raising children come across as bleak and dismal, let me remind you that being a parent is most often the source of great joy. But as in other arenas of life—falling in love, doing the polka, riding a roller coaster—the joy arises to the extent that you throw yourself into the experience. I've found that the crucial part comes in making the first and fundamental decision that raising your children well will be a top priority in your life. Once you've made a commitment to the question "What job will I do?" you'll realize tremendous freedom and divine joy that often arrive disguised as tasks, chores, and drudgery.

I feel sorry for parents who have yet to make the fundamental decision that raising their children well will be a top priority in their lives. No parent can claim to have been anything like perfect in carrying out this commitment. I certainly don't make any such claim to perfection. But if every demand your child's well-being makes on you becomes an inner crisis, ask yourself if you've freely committed to raising your child well over the long haul. People who end up taking better care of their cars or their cats or their careers than they take care of their kids need to think about what role their life and decisions have called them to.

In the foreword to her husband Stephen R. Covey's recent book, *The Seven Habits of Highly Effective Families,* Sandra Merrill Covey offered great wisdom for new, and veteran, parents. "Stephen once told a group of high-powered businessmen, 'If your company were falling apart, you know you'd do whatever you had to do to save it. Somehow you'd find a way. The same reasoning applies to your family. Most of us know what we need to do, but do we want to do it?'" Covey said he first developed his list of seven effective habits in the context of his own family life and later applied it to business. Surely some of these principles apply especially well to the vocation of raising a faith-filled family. The first principle, "Begin with the end in mind," which encourages families to focus on their mission, is a wise place to start. Tending to your child's faith is not something you can do divorced from tending to his or her other needs. Your mission, should you choose to accept it, is to tend to your whole child: body, mind, spirit, and soul.

I'm amazed at the people who think they can easily insert a child into the lifestyle they've become accustomed to. They seem to believe that with a minimum of disruption they will still be able to go to dinner with another couple at the drop of a hat. They will be able to continue to work the same long hours, finish up those reports at home, and spend Sunday morning lounging with the *New York Times*, eating brunch, and window-shopping. It doesn't work that way, and those who try to force it to are doing so at the risk of their child's emotional and spiritual welfare. When all is said and done, successful child rearing is not about technique but about commitment—commitment to provide for your own children's well-being. Raising kids with faith also means commitment—commitment to your own search for intimacy with God and your efforts to foster that relationship in your children as well.

The demands that workplaces put on employees today wreak havoc on families. You cannot schedule a child's needs in the same way you can lay out a day's schedule of work appointments. For many, work life is not conducive to family life and the practices that support family life. In the show-down between work and family, what typically suffer are many of the disciplines and practices that can ultimately make life worthwhile: easygoing time together, face-to-face time, church attendance, visits with extended family, and other religious practices or family rituals in the home.

ARE YOU PLAYING HIDE-AND-SEEK?

When time is tight and demands are high, raising kids can be seen as an endless series of chores. Or it can be seen as a wonderful way to spend a good portion of your life. Much depends on attitude and priorities.

For example, getting through a rainy Saturday with a couple of rambunctious toddlers is always going to be a challenge. If I feel that this is simply an unpleasant burden to endure until my real life can begin, I'm approaching it like a reluctant baby-sitter. It will be a long, long day.

I remember such Saturday mornings when my daughters were little. Often my first impulse was to try to skate by with doing the minimum. My plan was to simply endure. I'd hunker down on the couch, trying to read the paper, hoping that the cartoons would keep the girls quiet and occupied for the next four hours until lunch. It was miserable for them and for me!

My daughters could sense my aloofness, and it drove them crazy! My emotional withdrawal created a vacuum in our home. Since nature abhors a vacuum, the girls would fill it with taunting and teasing, crying and whining. My girls were quite capable of playing well on their own, but only if they were certain of parental presence. Then they felt secure in moving a short way away, where they would play contentedly, touching base regularly as they felt the need.

Tell a toddler, "Go away, you're bothering me," and she'll be all over you. The child's behavior will seem like pestering, but it's really a plea for connection. "Are you there? Do you see me? Can I count on you?"

Eventually the girls' pestering would bring me to my senses. The underlying message of all that acting up was "Hey, Dad, it's *you* we want." And I'd realize that I wanted them too. I'd get off the couch, sit down beside them, and talk to them eye-to-eye. I'd make jokes, play pretend games, build castles with the wooden blocks that were perpetually strewn about our living-room floor during those years, and be connected.

Then the tension would ease. Then the conflicts would evaporate. Then the good times would begin. The girls would cooperate if I needed to go to the hardware store or if there was a project I had to finish. The more I resisted playing my role as parent, the more they resisted my efforts to cajole them into "behaving." The more I showed up as the dad who cared, who took charge of the situation, the easier time we all had of it.

Paradoxically, those times when I realized that my higher goal was not to just endure but rather to give them my time, my attention, my guidance, a calm presence, good mental and physical nourishment, and interesting and purposeful things to do, such times were easy and delightful. Having come to that realization and made the decision to strive for my higher aims, I overcame the inertia of avoidance, and even though it took more energy to be proactive, in the end it seemed like less work. Life with your children can be one of nurturance and development—a fine starting ground for faith—rather than a series of battles and skirmishes.

Taking action ²

How to be a nurturing parent

State your intentions clearly. Stop and think about what you are committing to in the raising of your children. You might even put it in writing. Begin with the end in mind. Think ahead to the day your children are on their own. How would you define success as a parent of these children? What role will faith play in that vision of success? Compare notes with your spouse. Evaluate how equipped you are to make this happen. Remember Jesus' question to his would-be disciples: "Which of you, intending to build a tower, does not first sit down and estimate the cost, to see whether he has enough to complete it?"

Strengthen

your own faith. People tend to act out of either fear or faith. If faith is strong, fear diminishes (and vice versa). Becoming a parent can be a tremendous spur to your own faith. Having a child puts you in intimate touch with mystery, awe, simple trust, the need for mercy, and, above all, overwhelming love. This is the stuff that our own faith is made of. Welcoming a child into your life can be a most religious response to life.

Keep good companions. To keep that faith alive through the many years of ups and downs as life unfolds, it helps to surround yourself with others who share your values. Many in our culture don't value the practice of religious faith (even though most will give lip service to the idea). Many don't value the importance of nurturing a child's development. Ours can be a very individualistic culture, with not a lot of support given to the concept that small persons have claims on us and are worth subordinating our own wants, and even needs, for. Find people whose attitudes and life choices support your highest values. If you don't live what you believe, you will, over time, come to believe what you live.

A place where I have found people whose values I admire and share is at church. Surely not everyone who attends church is a model parent or a model Christian, but I'm more likely to find people with values similar to mine at church than, say, at the racetrack or the country club.

Watch your language. How

we talk to ourselves about the tasks involved in being a parent can help too. Do you want to make a quick improvement in your attitude throughout the day? Change the way you talk about yourself and your duties. For example, don't moan, "I *have* to pick up the kids from volleyball." Rather you can try, "I get the chance to spend time with my kids while I drive them home from volleyball." Does that seem like a distinction without a difference? Just try it. Instead of "I *have* to clean the house for visitors," say, "I get to prepare the house for fun with guests." Having an optimistic outlook has an impact on your attitude, but you're also more

likely to find the good that's in every situation and savor it. Your children, who are always observing, will also benefit greatly from this positive approach to living.

And while you're at it, don't grumble, "C'mon, kids, we *have* to go to church." Instead say, "Let's go worship God with our neighbors and friends."

Ask your children

what they hope for, spiritually, from life. We often ask our children what they want to be when they grow up. We don't expect an analytical answer, but we hope to get a glimpse of their interests and hopes. Why not also ask them what they'd like their spiritual life to be like when they're grown? Invite them to think about what their spiritual development might mean to them. What are their spiritual hopes? Don't leave your children's spiritual aspirations out of the equation.

There are many ways to take up this question profitably with your children. When my daughters were quite young, I would periodically ask them if they had any questions they would like to ask God. I heard some surprising ideas, ranging from the mundane ("Hey, Mr. God, why do you let it rain on Saturdays?") to the profound ("Why did Mrs. Sullivan [an older parishioner who befriended us] have to go to a nursing home?"). I'd wait until I was alone with one of the girls and ask the question when the two of us had time on our hands, like when we were waiting in the car for my wife to pick up a few things from the store. I tried not to badger them with the questions and would back off as soon as the exercise became tiresome for them. But I always found it worth the asking.

Here's another approach. *Life* magazine once ran a delightful photo story titled "Kids' Pictures to God." The magazine's editors gave a camera to each of fifty-six budding photojournalists, ages eight to thirteen, and asked them to tackle three tough questions: Who is God? What would you ask God if you could? And how would you show that in a photograph? The photos were amazing, and it's a creative way for you to get a glimpse of where your children's mind and imagination are regarding God and faith. If you don't trust your children with the family's good camera, pick up

a disposable one as a summer or weekend project when they say they're bored.

Ask God for help. Prayer has been one of the biggest helps to me in being a father. Sincere prayer can help clarify your hopes for your children so that your plans will not be filled with ego or fear. Prayer can help you stop and examine other, more creative ways to respond to problems when you're ready to act in anger or frustration. Prayer is a way to be put back in touch with your deepest desires for the well-being of your children.

As a parent, I take great comfort in the example of St. Monica, long-suffering mother of St. Augustine. Her son became one of the leading lights in Christianity, a saint of great passion and influence, a father of the church. But he certainly didn't begin that way. Though his mother was devout, Augustine was content to live a determinedly faithless life of public sinning. Monica implored her son, cajoled him, pleaded with him to repent and convert, all to no avail. And she prayed. Though her plans and schemes to change her son's wayward ways failed miserably, her prayers had great effect. Year after year she continued to pray for his soul, and in time those prayers were answered. As much as Augustine might have tried to resist her direct attempts to change him, he could not resist the lure of God's love that inspired all her years of prayer for his conversion. That love won out, and Monica's prayers were answered.

Call on the example of faithful relatives, living and dead. Often there are people in our family who can inspire us to strength and courage, generosity and kindness. I often think of my four grandparents, each of whom came to the U.S. from Ireland as a teenager. When my own daughter turned sixteen and I was nervous about her getting behind the wheel of a car and driving a mile to McDonald's with her friends, it really hit home that both my grandmothers left their homes, never to return again, at that same tender age. My mother's mom knew no one in Chicago, yet she scrambled to find work, get married,

raise a family, and also continue to support her family back in Ireland. At my grandmother's wake, one of the distant cousins came up to tell that when he arrived penniless in Chicago decades before, she had a suit of clothes, some money, and the address of a potential employer awaiting him. "And I surely wasn't the first, nor the last poor bloke, who knew such generosity from her." She worked as a maid at some of Chicago's fancy hotels. Whenever I travel, especially on business, and stay at a big, fancy hotel, I think of the grueling hours she put in, and I am profoundly grateful for her sacrifice. She is a model of faith chosen and lived out over many days.

Seek progress, not perfection. Making a commitment is for the long haul and should not be easily thrown over when you hit a bump in the road or momentarily fail. In this era when pop psychology is so much the rage, some parents fear that one wrong move will result in such trauma that their child will spend endless years dealing with it in therapy. In fact, one of my friends reports that when she "blows it" with one of her kids she sighs and says, "Don't worry, I'll write all this down for your therapist. It'll save you months of payments years from now."

But keep things in perspective. Every parent messes up, just as every human being messes up. The value of making the major, central commitment to do the best job you can is that you're building a history with this child. Your child knows that you may not be perfect but that you can be relied upon over the long haul. God willing, you'll have a long life together with many opportunities. Even if you get lost along the way, if you keep your main intention clear in your mind, you'll continue to find your way back to your path.

Get help if you

need it. I once attended an intensive leadership-development course that closed with a segment on "factors that derail a promising career." The research identified the behaviors and traits that most often trip up potential business leaders. Interestingly, most of the factors cited have little to do with

technical business or management skills. Mostly what tripped people up were personality defects—such as hypercompetitiveness, insecurity, difficulty in communicating, or bad habits regarding managing time or handling moods.

Likewise for parents, the obstacles we face are typically not the technical aspects of parenting—knowing how to give clear, consistent messages to our kids, how to transition easily from playtime to bedtime, etc. No, it's the larger character or personality flaws and the issues not dealt with that have the largest negative impact on the job we do as parents.

For some, it's a matter of failure to learn new habits. We learn how to be parents from the way we were reared. For good or for ill, our most natural way to treat children is the way the adults in our lives, particularly our parents, treated us. For most of us, as it will be for our own children, that's a mixed bag. For example, your parents may have been excellent at setting clear expectations for you but were aloof and ill attuned to your emotional state. Or maybe your parents were always ready to listen but not good at setting limits. It's likely that unless you make a choice in the matter, you will do as was done unto you. Maybe you'll repeat that behavior; or maybe the pendulum will swing and you'll over-react and do the opposite. But the treatment you received will be a deter-mining factor in how you treat your own children.

Many of these traits can change easily with awareness, patience, gentle-ness with yourself, and persistence. But there are times when, no matter how hard we try, on our own we cannot seem to alter patterns that we know aren't working for us and our children. At times like these it's important to get whatever help we need. My friend Mike says, "If you keep on doing what you *don't* want to do, or can't start doing what you *do* want to do, it's time to get help." A committed parent will be willing to get whatever help is necessary. Stephen R. Covey's assertion to busi-ness executives comes to mind again: If this were your business, you'd find out what needed to be done and call on every possible resource to do it.

DOES FAITH TALK SCARE YOU JUST A LITTLE?

It's common for parents to feel uneasy talking to their children about sex. But I think many of us also find it difficult to talk with our children about faith. Like sex, faith is a very personal topic, and a powerful one. And just as our feelings about sex can be complex, powerful, and even ambivalent, so too with matters of personal faith. But the opportunity to talk with our children about these topics can truly help them grow up well.

Before we can make room for the thoughts, beliefs, and feelings of our children, we need to become comfortable with our own. Usually our trepidation is a sign that we're clinging to old beliefs or an amalgam of ideas that don't quite fit together and wouldn't bear too much scrutiny. But once we have worked through that, our conversations about faith (as well as about sex) can be rich, thoughtful, faithful, and valuable for all involved.

One caution for parents: You must realize that you cannot control others—even your children. And when it comes to faith, this is as it should be. Faith comes to each individual as a gift from God. I can't *bestow* faith on my children. But I do hope to be in a position to influence them. As the late Henri Nouwen wrote, "We cannot change people by our convictions, . . . advice, and proposals, but we can offer a space where people are encouraged to listen with attention and care to the voices speaking in their own center." Learn to speak from your own heart about faith (whether in words or in actions). It will speak to the heart of your child as well. Here's a prayer I wrote that first appeared in *At Home with Our Faith*, a newsletter designed to nurture the spirituality of families.

Real Presence

Let my heart be a wide and welcome harbor
where my children come to rest.
May these arms stretch wide and strong
to hold his fear, her hurt, their tattered sense of self.

May there be a solidness within me
on which their pain may crash
and recede
and I remain.

Let my presence be an island to them
in storm-tossed seasons,
rising up from troubled waters to offer
shelter, respite, and firm dry ground.

May they find in me
a haven to tend to battered souls
until the day the certainty of such solid ground
launches them to sail uncharted waters unafraid.

DO YOU NEED A SECOND CHANCE?

A woman at a church meeting once shared a story that illustrates my point.

> Last night I got a "homesick" call about 10:00 P.M.
> from my daughter, who's away at college. That may
> not seem like an amazing thing, but a dozen years
> ago I would never have imagined I'd be living this
> long, let alone be awake and coherent enough to lis-
> ten to my daughter's problems responsibly at ten
> o'clock at night. You see, twelve years ago I had not

43

yet begun my recovery from alcoholism. In fact, early each evening I would slip into crying fits, bemoaning the plight of my daughter, who we adopted, and wondering why she couldn't have been given a mother who was responsible, loving, attentive, and caring. Back then it never crossed my mind that the responsible, loving, attentive, and caring mother she needed could be me. Such was my despair and my misery.

Thankfully, I found a program of recovery. Since then, one day at a time, I have become not a perfect mother but a darned good one, one that my daughter can rely on—day or night. I found a way to become the mother I always hoped she would have.

So, begin with the end in mind. If you want to play a significant role in introducing your child to faith in a gracious God who keeps his eye on the sparrow, commit from the start to make family life your spiritual path. Realize that you are entering into a relationship of mystery. Tend to your own emotional and spiritual health. Be attuned to your child's needs at each stage of development. Attend to your own relationship with God, and open yourself to whatever grace God offers through life in your family to become a whole and holy person. It's a joyful path if you walk it with your heart and soul undivided.

Like many parents before you, you may wonder whether you have the wherewithal to handle the job of parent. Rest assured that you most certainly do. The words of O. Hobart Mowrer come to mind: "You alone can do it; but you cannot do it alone." Fortunately, you don't have to do it alone. Jesus said, "I will not leave you orphans." On our spiritual path we have the presence of God, the example of Jesus, and the guidance of the Holy Spirit. We have the community of believers to support us and the spiritual practices and disciplines of the ages to show the way. And most of all, we have our children, who are our most important, and possibly most effective, teachers and spiritual guides.

A Closer Look

Especially for Dads

Social scientists continue to report that many Americans, male and female, suffer from a "father hunger." Growing up, they didn't have sufficient experience of connection with their fathers. Dads worked away from the home—sometimes long hours—and often felt out of place in the mix of family life. Business success and the demands of being the main provider came at a great price for men in the fifties, sixties, and seventies. Many men sacrificed their awareness of just how fiercely they loved their children and how much they wanted to be close to them. In time, the distance increased, and the awareness grew more and more dim.

I always wondered what my dad thought of me.

A high school sophomore

Dads, it is essential that you do not let this grand and wonderful desire to be a good father wither and die from lack of attention. Be proactive in this regard. Take steps to reconnect with your feelings and communicate them to your children. I wrote this suggestion in a June issue of *U.S. Catholic* that came out just in time for Father's Day.

Imagine this: You pull open a drawer one morning, and way in the back under those paisley socks you haven't worn in about a dozen years, you find a packet of letters. You look them over, and it turns out they are from your dad—letters he wrote you years ago, and you somehow forgot about them. Wouldn't you stop everything, sit down on the edge of the bed, and read every word? I would.

Fathers, so would your kids. Americans may admire men who are the strong, silent type, but they also feel the brunt of that silence. In a time when kids are bombarded by thousands of advertising messages a day, it's not time for fathers to take the Fifth. This Father's Day, do yourself and your kids a favor: Communicate on paper. You may produce words that will last a lifetime—theirs, not yours.

I hear a lot of people talk about their lives, and many (men especially) talk ruefully of the emotional emptiness they feel when they think about their fathers. They may sense love there but also a big question mark. "What did he feel?" "What was he thinking?" "What did he stand for?" "What did I mean to him, if anything?"

What makes that pervasive sense of emptiness all the more poignant is that it's often so obvious to others that fathers have an enormous storehouse of emotion for their children. This was made abundantly clear when I attended the annual father-daughter dance at my elder daughter's school. As always, the dance was a fun event where proud papas spent time with their daughters. It had all the makings of a truly anachronistic occasion, but trust me, it's a delightful tradition. At one point in the evening, the DJ (whose job it was to see that all of us dads made total fools of ourselves) lined up the men on one side of the dance floor and our daughters on the other. The DJ challenged us to a singing contest to see whether dads or daughters could sing the loudest. This competition brought out the feistiness in the daughters, which simply melted the competitiveness of all the dads. I looked around at my fellow singers and was touched at how glowingly these men—firemen, carpenters, salesmen, and cops—looked at their daughters. They stood misty-eyed, beaming, dumbstruck with pride. I wondered how many of them would remain dumbstruck when it came to telling their daughters—and their other children at home—just how much they treasure them.

SHOW REAL STRENGTH

In her book *The Goodness of Ordinary People* (Crown, 1996), Faith Middleton retold stories she has heard over the years on her popular National Public Radio program. One caller told this touchingly sad tale.

> When my father died thirty-eight years ago, we were not terribly close. He was a remote man who found it difficult to express his emotions. But we had one tradition that I will always remember because it taught me a lot about overcoming fear. Something about the power of thunderstorms attracted him. Whenever there was a thunderstorm he'd throw open the screen and stand at the window with his elbows on the windowsill and just watch. I was very excited one day when he sort of invited me to stand with him. As time went on watching the storm and the beautiful lightning, we kind of moved a little closer to each other until our elbows were touching. We'd stand there and watch the storm, not saying anything, and I think it was the only closeness we ever really had. To this day, whenever there's a thunderstorm, I stand in the window.

Nice, but I think that dad could have done better than that. Gentlemen, find a way.

What holds us back? Is it genetic? cultural? a missing enzyme or hormone? the momentum of history? Whatever it is, it's time to rewrite this portion of gender history, one letter at a time.

For some people, there's nothing more intimidating than a blank page. So how do you start? You can think of a quality that's special about your child, something you admire in him or her. Think about a time you really felt joy in being his or her dad. Put it down on paper just as you would tell an understanding friend. You don't have to get flowery. Simple and straightforward is the key. You could start by writing, "I really admire the way you . . ." or "I've always enjoyed it when you . . ." or "I've always been able to count on you to . . ." or "You really made me proud the day you . . ."

Let that be just the start. Maybe there's more you want to say. Describe what it was like the day she was born. Tell how proud his grandpa was on his baptism day. Tell how she came to have the name you gave her. Keep on writing. Tell him things you've always wanted to tell: what you consider most important in life, what your hopes are, how family has helped you get through the good times and the bad.

You can tell her how her grandparents came to this country and what a sacrifice they made for those to come later. Describe your worst job and what it taught you about the value of persistence and education. If you live by words of wisdom, put them down on paper. This letter won't neces- sarily come easy, even to people who write for a living. Don't make too big a thing of it. This is not Shakespeare or a Pulitzer-winning essay. It's just a chance to pass on a legacy to your child that no one can take away.

Well, if words absolutely won't come, don't despair. Take a half hour or forty-five minutes and go to a card shop.

This time, walk past the joke cards and go to the ones that express some real sentiment. Take time to read through the cards until you find at least one that says something you feel. Purchase the card, but do more than just sign your name at the bottom. Write at least one original line, something like "This card expresses how I feel about you" or "I hope you know I'm proud of you."

Don't worry if your child is too young. Write the letter and store it away. It will make a good present during those early teen years when a parent's job is to be dorky and wrong. And don't use the excuse that your children don't live with you. They will always be your children; will you always be their dad?

So, this Father's Day, turn off the golf. When they ask what you want, tell them you want an hour alone. Spend that hour in front the computer, at the kitchen table, on a patio chair, or at your workbench putting down one word after another, telling each one of your children something you've always wanted to say but never found the time. Now *is* the time.

Not that they'll stop everything and read it. Most likely they'll push the note into a pocket or slide it under a comic book or a video-game cartridge. But sometime down the line, your child will come across that letter in the bottom of a sock drawer, put everything else aside, and read every word. Can you ask for a better Father's Day gift than that?

WRITE FROM THE HEART

- Don't compare this child to anyone else in the family. Don't even mention anyone else in a comparative way.
- Don't say, "Mother and I . . ." Speak for yourself.

- Don't offset a positive with a negative ("We all know you don't have the best temper in the world, but I like the way you make your bed" or "Even though you ruined my power drill, I'm proud you made a touchdown against those darn Wildcats").

- Don't worry that you'll spoil them, no matter what age they are.

- Don't worry that the letter will get emotional. You can take it; so can your child.

- Don't worry about your spelling, grammar, punctuation, or vocabulary. Look beyond that. They will.

- Don't put it off. "Now is the acceptable time," says the Lord. Do you want your only legacy to be those old paisley socks?

*Effective communication
within any tradition is always
a matter of one generation
holding the next to its heart.*

JOHN SHEA

CHAPTER FOUR

Relationships, Messages, and Clues

Means of Handing Down a Heritage

Years ago, I learned a lesson about passing on religious faith during a golden summer while my family was on vacation. My daughters were young, about ages three and six, and we were staying with my wife's extended family in a spacious summer home just a short walk from Lake Michigan's beautiful shoreline. The days were filled with lively conversations and stories and simple meals featuring good food and lots of laughter. We played endless card games on the deck on sunny afternoons or at the long kitchen table well into the evenings. Most of all, I remember lazy hours when my wife and I played with our daughters in the sun and sand.

One sunny afternoon I went to get my daughters up from their naps so that we could head down for an afternoon at the beach, but they weren't in their beds. And they weren't in the living room or in the kitchen or on the deck. I began to worry, knowing that the lake was just a half block away. I was about to call out for them when I passed by the room where Aunt Marie was staying. I heard familiar whispering and glimpsed slight movement, so I stopped and peeked into the room.

Sitting on the edge of the bed was Aunt Marie, with Judy and Patti plopped on either side of her. Marie was holding a well-worn prayer book jammed full of holy cards. The girls' eyes were wide with curiosity. I listened in on their hushed whisperings. "Now, this is your great-great-grandmother's," said Aunt Marie, holding a prayer card in her hand. "She died just a few days before Dennis was married. She baked the best bread and cakes and was always one for helping a sick neighbor or someone down on their luck.

"And this one's from old Mrs. Clancy. She was a great help to our mother after Father passed away. And here's a prayer card for Father Sheehy. He was a wonderful priest. He went off to the missions in Bolivia. He always spoke so lovingly about the people there."

As she talked, she'd hand off a card to the girls. They'd hold them reverently in their tiny hands, looking at them front and back. "And now let's pray for the people I promised to pray for," said Aunt Marie. The three of them bowed their heads as she began a litany that included neighbors, troubled relatives, poor souls in purgatory, shopkeepers, the congregation of nuns who taught her years ago, and deceased family members. As always, she ended her prayer with, "God help the sick."

I left them to their prayers and stood out on the deck appreciating the fine day. In a few minutes the girls came dashing out, towels in hand, eager to go to the beach. We were a motley caravan traipsing down to the shoreline with plastic rafts, inner tubes, beach chairs, and blankets. Young and old, we went off to the water.

The waves were high that day, and I sat for a while watching as Aunt Marie and Uncle Johnny walked the girls into the surf. There they were, hand in hand, laughing as the waves crashed into them. Clinging together, they stood, holding one another up as the currents pushed and pulled them. They were safe, hanging on together.

RELATIONSHIPS FROM GENERATION TO GENERATION

I was on vacation, so I didn't give it much deep thought. But the image of them holding on to one another in the turbulent lake stayed with me, and it stays with me still as a moment rich in meaning and depth. I share it now because it contains so many elements I believe are essential to passing on a living faith.

Setting

The extended family is where life is lived fully and passionately. Children often get their sense of what life is all about in interactions with extended family. These are people who are connected to you, have claims on you (and you on them), and would even die for you. You place your own story in the context of this larger story. "What's life all about?" "What do we believe in?" "What do we stand for?" "Who am I?" All these questions get answered first in light of your place in your larger family.

And it's true that children can hear and absorb from others the truths that they become oblivious to when spoken by their parents. As a manager, I know this is true in the workplace as well. I've learned that it's wise to send employees off to seminars to learn from others what I could probably tell them. But they're more likely to believe something when they hear it from an "expert." Likewise, we parents know that a beloved outsider can impress truths on our children that they would dismiss from us. Grandparents, aunts and uncles, godparents, and valued family friends can have a major impact for good on our children. These are deeply formative relationships.

Close relationships with extended family members are major sources of strength that families are losing in American society and culture. When I watch recent immigrants—for example, Hispanic families—I observe the obvious importance of the grandparents, especially the *abuelitas* (grandmothers), in nurturing the faith of the youngsters. This can be done directly through instruction but also (and probably more powerfully over the long haul) through the subtle, everyday interactions between the grandparents and the children.

I know that one of the most powerful teaching moments in my life was the annual Thanksgiving feast at Grandma's. The whole day was hectic and happily chaotic. There must have been fifty people laughing and talking in that small home on May Street. But when the turkey and potatoes and green beans and sweet potatoes and rolls and Jell-O mold and turnips (the list goes on) were all on the table, the hilarity stopped. A hush fell over the entire group, even us little cousins consigned to the overflow seating in the side bedroom. And then we prayed. We all knew the same prayer: "Bless us, O Lord, and these thy gifts. . . ." What a day of powerful lessons.

Later, when the ancients were playing poker and we'd sidle up to our fathers to stack the nickels and dimes, the murmured conversation, thick with the flavor of Tipperary, would as naturally include talk of work at the gas company or rail yards, as snippets of a decent sermon or doings up at the parish. Around the room were not only Grandma and Grandpa and Auntie Bridget and Uncle Leo but also, gazing steadily from their spots on the dining-room wall, the Sacred Heart and the Blessed Mother.

If, when the larger family gets together, you say grace before meals or worship together or naturally, even subtly, highlight the religious component of the event, the lesson will be learned. The message is "This is who we are. We are people for whom faith matters. We make it a part of our times together."

Another factor that made the incident at Lake Michigan so powerful and illustrative is how naturally the lesson evolved. Praying while poring over her prayer book was a normal event in Aunt Marie's life. She was letting the girls in on an activity of great meaning that was part of her day. This was not a put-on or a show. It wasn't someone saying to herself, "Let's devise a lesson in prayer for these kids." Rather, she was inviting them to an experience of her daily life. As is typical with those who have attained spiritual depth, Marie naturally desires to give away freely what was given to her and what she has come to treasure. Part of the lesson my daughters learned that day was that it's a good thing to pray for others daily; this is something a respected person eagerly does.

Content

The lesson was delivered in terms of relationships, commitments, love, and service. It wasn't about who put on the best act at being holy but about the lives people lived and the ways in which their faith illuminated those lives. There was nothing grand or theoretical. The lesson was simple and concrete.

Yet the content is far ranging, embracing all aspects of life. Marie prayed for everyone she encountered, from the grocer to the pope, from the newest child born in the family to the older folks lingering near death. She prayed for people taking driver's tests, a nephew hoping for a promotion, or a neighbor awaiting the results of medical tests for cancer. There was no place and no part of life that went untouched by grace or went unoffered up to God's healing touch. No moment of Marie's day and no part of her heart were outside the gaze of God. The content of Marie's lesson was "Everything belongs in God's hands."

Method

During this show-and-tell, the girls were exposed to a number of lessons. First, Marie's old prayer book was a longtime companion. They knew that they were walking with her down a well-traveled path. This prayer time happened daily, like meals are taken daily. The prayer cards they held in their hands had vivid pictures of Mary, Jesus, the holy family, and Archangel Michael victorious over Satan. The words and the pictures were both evocative and rich. The litany of prayers focused on people and events that were concrete, specific, and real.

The lesson wasn't a lecture; it was a joyful invitation to "come and see." My daughters were being offered not only information but also a way of living that leads to the abundant life Jesus promises. Marie offered an interactive experience wherein she let the kids see, touch, hear, and "handle the goods." Her own enthusiasm and sincere faith were perhaps the biggest lesson of all. Faith is spread not by teachers but by witnesses.

Reinforcement

When we all went down to the beach, the girls got an additional lesson. The waves were high and could be dangerous. But Aunt Marie and Uncle Johnny were there to hang on to. In fact, by grabbing hands and hanging on, they could walk straight into those waves, laughing and rejoicing. Together, we survive. Today, years later, Marie and Johnny are a bit wobbly on their feet. It was just last Sunday that my daughters were escorting their great-aunt and great-uncle up our front stairs as they came to celebrate another family gathering. And though, this time, Marie and Johnny were leaning on my girls for support, I know that the girls will lean on the strength and character of these, their elders, throughout their entire lives.

I feel grateful that my girls have been exposed to faith lessons from so many of their extended family members over the years. Occasionally I'll hear young parents complain about having to spend time visiting relatives. They talk about the situation as a burden rather than an opportunity. And from a distance, I cannot judge their situation. But I hope they are not being too quick to eliminate valuable relationships from their child's life that can be crucial to the child's future faith.

It may have been stifling in the old days for families to spend every Sunday at Grandma's. But have we eliminated a valuable element of our own lives and the lives of our children by all but cutting off ties with extended family members?

Almost everyone agrees that religion is best nurtured at home. But too often we make the mistake of thinking that we need to import classroom methods to teach these lessons. This is odd because teachers are doing all they can to employ real-life lessons in the classroom. They know that such real-life lessons are the ones that make the most lasting impression on students.

LESSONS FROM REAL LIFE

My wife, Kathleen, teaches math to seventh-graders, which to me seems to be an extremely brave calling. She's constantly trying to devise ways to bring real-life examples to introduce and illustrate math principles. For example, she'll have her students work in teams on such projects as investing ten thousand dollars (with imaginary money, of course) in the stock market. Together they decide what to invest, how to calculate profit and loss, how to compare results with others, and so on. The lessons become more than abstract theory. After their own experience and observation, the students are better prepared to catch the theory and retain it. The kids engage their imaginations, their personalities, and their whole minds in the project. Other hands-on lessons involve using blocks to estimate area and volume and playing games of chance to learn about probability. Kathleen is not alone in these efforts to involve more of the person in the classroom. Throughout her district and in schools across the country, teachers in all subjects are working to make their classrooms more interactive and reality based.

Kathleen attended a seminar about how to help students retain more of what they learn. She received the following list. I can't vouch for the accuracy of these percentages, but the principles are surely true.

People retain

- 10% of what they *read*
- 20% of what they *hear*
- 30% of what they *see*
- 50% of what they *see and hear*
- 70% of what they *say*
- 90% of what they *do and say*

That last statistic is good news for parents who make the effort to introduce faith to their children. Any efforts you make to communicate your faith to your children are bound to deepen your own spiritual life in the process.

Understanding how children learn to grasp complex concepts will help you foster development of your children's faith. Children move from the simple and concrete to the more complex and abstract. For example, it's only when a child learns what it feels like to "fall down and go boom" that he or she can go on to develop an understanding of the concept of gravity. Likewise, having regular experience of a family meal can be the prelude to understanding the Eucharist, just as experiencing forgiveness and acceptance after hurting another family member can lead the way to understanding the theology of repentance and redemption.

We do not approach the study of faith with a blank slate. We bring our life experiences as the raw material from which to build a human faith in a God who became human. Our children's earliest brushes with the holy and the sacred, experienced in ordinary, daily life, become the building blocks for developing an adult faith.

In *Magical Child* (Plume, 1992), the groundbreaking book about child development, Joseph Chilton Pearce established that all higher knowledge grows from and depends on early, concrete experiences. He wrote, "All thinking arises out of concreteness, which means out of the brain patterns resulting from actual body movements of interacting with actual things."

Thus, a child learns what Mom means by "Hot, don't touch" as a prelude to grasping laws of thermodynamics. Likewise, a child gains clues about God's faithfulness by experiencing a parent's reliability, or about God's mercy when siblings offer forgiveness when the child says, "I'm sorry." Too often we think of religious education as a mysterious process that takes place at church or later in life. The truth is that the foundation of our children's later faith is being laid in the day-to-day life we share with them today. The more we're aware of this truth, the more we can enrich their experiences and point to clues about God's life and goodness all around them.

IMAGINATION FOR THE DAY TO DAY

Christians tend to look for these signs of God in the world we inhabit. Some faiths believe that the world is evil, that we should try to become pure in spirit and turn our backs on the world. But for Catholics that's heresy. We believe that the world is good and that through our daily interactions in the world we can come to experience the divine.

Seeing clues to God in the world is what theologians call the analogical imagination. Believers who have analogical imagination tend to emphasize the similarities, rather than the differences, between God and creation. Everything that exists is a metaphor for God. This is a particularly Catholic way of looking at life and creation. There's a family resemblance between creation and the Creator. In everything that is, God shines through. St. Bonaventure said that "everything shows the *vestigia Dei*—the fingerprints and footprints of God."

I like that, the thought that everything has the fingerprints of God all over it. Even you and I bear the fingerprints of God. God is that close to us.

Jesus knew that we learn to see God's reality by analogy. That's why he used parables: "The kingdom of heaven is like a banquet," "is like a woman who lost a coin and then found it," "is a pearl of great price that someone found in a field." The New Testament is packed with imagery pointing to God, helping to train our vision so that we might see more clearly.

Father Richard Rohr said that this view—the analogical imagination—professes that there's no absolute distinction between the sacred and the profane. There is not natural and supernatural. There's only one world, and it's shot through with the supernatural. The analogical imagination, in Rohr's view, gives one a sense of belonging to the universe. And as it turns out, God sent the Son to validate that God is present among us. The most radical experience of creation revealing God is Jesus.

So now it makes sense to me that when I was growing up, many people had Mary altars and holy-water fonts in the home. Our Polish and Slavic neighbors brought their Easter baskets to the church to be blessed on Holy Saturday. We had a Sacred Heart statue on the dashboard of our car, we made the sign of the cross at the sound of sirens, and we knew that God lived in our home—walked our halls, sat at our kitchen table, and watched over us as we slept. My fingerprints may have been on the refrigerator door, but God's fingerprints were all over the house.

As the Jesuit poet Gerard Manley Hopkins wrote in the poem "God's Grandeur":

> The world is charged with the grandeur of God.
>> It will flame out, like shining from shook foil;
>> It gathers to a greatness, like the ooze of oil
> Crushed. . . .

Thus, our experiences within the home, in our earliest and most formative relationships, are the first clues to who God is, who we are, what the nature of the world is, and what's expected of us. And parents greatly affect their children's capacity to see God—for good or for ill.

THE MESSAGES KIDS HEAR FROM US

A story might make this parental influence more clear.

I taught high school religion for a number of years. I really enjoyed the opportunity it afforded me to get to know the students. It was a real laboratory in which to study the development of faith in young people. Because of the variety and importance of topics we'd discuss in class, I came to know and understand a lot about the freshness and tenderness of the faith of these young people.

Teenagers may appear not at all interested in the spiritual aspect of their lives, but I learned that just the opposite is true. Despite outward indications to the contrary, faith meant a great deal to these kids, and they were struggling to make sense of their world and come to understand how God fit into it. I came to believe that, at heart, we're all interested in the central questions about faith, about God, and about our moral purpose in this life. The kids often resisted and rebelled against standard religious practice, but they were, each in a unique way, very taken up in the quest for a relationship with God. I believe that's as true today as it was back then.

In my Scripture class one day, we got to the section in Matthew 6, where Jesus instructs his disciples to pray the Our Father. I was waxing eloquent (or so I imagined) on the wisdom and simplicity of the prayer, about how Jesus had really made it easy for us to pray by including so many human concerns in this model for prayer: daily bread, gratitude, forgiveness, and avoidance of temptation. I emphasized how Jesus had helped us in prayer by addressing his words not to a distant, omnipotent, and hidden God but to "our Father." I went on and on about how radical a concept it was to see God as our Father and what a joy it is to be able to approach God that way.

And, as usual while I taught, my students were doodling, surreptitiously doing their math homework, passing notes about an upcoming dance, or staring blankly into space. But I noticed that Mary was upset. She had a scowl on her pretty, young face and was grinding her pencil back and forth on her notebook, making a thick, black mark in the margin.

After class, I tried to connect with her, but she looked down and brushed her way past me. As she left, I said, "Hey,

I'd really like to know what's going on. Did something I say upset you?" She kept walking.

I learned to be alert to such a reaction in class. I also learned something of why people who do pastoral work over a long period of time most often operate from compassion rather than dogma. Frequently, seemingly harmless topics I brought up in class could set off a "depth charge" in one of the kids. And sometimes I was privileged to hear what was going on in those depths.

I recognized that something that had gone on in class had deeply affected Mary. She was clearly in pain. Yet I couldn't imagine what had caused it. After all, I'd been talking about Jesus' most welcome news: that we could approach God as a loving father. What could be wrong with that?

After school, I ran into Mary. I pulled her into a classroom and said, "You're upset. What's going on?"

She sat for a moment looking down, tears welling up in her eyes. Then it came: "You wouldn't want to say the Our Father if you had a father like mine."

I sat in silence, awareness beginning to dawn on me. She poured out a story of a man who had emotionally abused her and her mother for years. He was a man apparently full of fear and hate who attempted to control everything and everybody in his life. He was openly unfaithful to the mother, harsh and demeaning to his daughter. He ridiculed her every success; he told her that she looked ugly and that no one would ever want her. It was amazing to me that after hearing all this, she could function so well in school and in life. She was a delightful young woman. Yet within her I could now see the pain, the block of solid ice in the core of her heart. I was angry at her father for taking so much away from his daughter: her sense of self-worth, her trust, and her ability to open up to life. And I was terribly angry that he took away her ability to see God as good and loving. In her mind, God the Father would be like all fathers (or at least like her father): aloof, untrustworthy, vindictive, demeaning, and jealous.

THE CLUES KIDS NEED FROM US

Like all human beings, Mary was seeking God by using what she had to work with. Jesus understood this. He said, "How close am I to you? Here, how about as close to you as this bread you eat?" What's God like? God is like the good shepherd who seeks out the lost among his flock. God is like a man who threw a banquet and invited people from the highways and byways. God is like a father who stood on a hill, anxiously longing for his errant son's return.

But sometimes these natural pointers to the divine, these clues, get twisted. Hearing Mary's story helped me understand why Jesus said it would be better for a person to have a millstone tied to his neck and be thrown into the sea than to spoil a young person's ability to see and understand who God is and how God loves us.

How important is family life in preparing the ground for faith to grow? Victoria Lee Erickson, a professor at Drew University, said, "All we ever need to know in life is learned in families before we get to kindergarten." This is as true of faith as it is for learning our colors and numbers and how to say please and thank you. We are introduced to God through the workings of our analogical imagination. We see God not through abstract theory but by analogy in the traces we find in the here and now.

Parents have a great opportunity to provide those connections and create the right atmosphere. We can both point to the clues and, through our loving care of our children, actually *be* clues to God's identity and presence. We don't have to put on a Holy Roller act to achieve this. We simply do what loving parents do.

Our children learn about God when they receive tender care when they're sick. They learn about God's love when they see delight for themselves in our eyes. They get a taste of God's prodigious generosity when they wake up to find gifts from Santa under the Christmas tree. They're prepared to trust in the constancy of God when we are reliably there for them. They learn about God's wisdom when we show prudence in determining boundaries for their actions. In our mundane, everyday relating, we either reveal God or, as in the case of Mary's father, obscure the face of God from our child's sight.

The spiritual task of parents begins when they prepare a space for their child, not only in their house or apartment, but most especially in their lives. It begins when a mother (like Elizabeth, mother of John the Baptist) hears the news that she is "with child" and when joy enlivens the baby within her womb.

The spiritual task of parents continues from the early days of receiving and bonding, through nurturing and coddling, through training and explaining, correcting and encouraging, consoling and connecting, and, at every stage, practicing letting go. The key is to live fully in each of these stages, alert, aware, and awake to your child as well as alert, aware, and awake to God's presence.

How do you, through your habits and traditions, bring, in Robert Wuthnow's words, "the daily round of family activities . . . into the presence of God"? Here, and in subsequent chapters, are some ways you might consider in order to cultivate your children's faith and your own analogical imagination.

Taking action 3

How to uncover your family's spiritual dimension

Cultivate relations with extended family. Have your children quiz their great-aunts and great-uncles and grandparents on what their faith means to them. You can get at it in roundabout ways. For example, ask them if they remember where they were baptized or received their first communion. Did they ever want to be a nun or a priest? If they emigrated from a foreign country, do they recall memories or customs they enjoyed in their homeland? Who is their favorite saint, and why did they name their children the way they did? Encourage the older generation to practice their customs with their grandchildren and great-grandchildren.

Share your own religious practices with your children in as natural a way as possible. If you have a devotion or a religious practice that means a lot to you, let your children know. Invite them to participate with you. My wife begins each day with a time of quiet meditation and reflective writing in her journal. Our daughter Patti has followed her lead in journal writing—though Patti's reflection time arrives at the end of the day.

Treat everyday objects in the home as holy vessels. Benedictine sister Joan Chittister wrote a great book, *Wisdom Distilled from the Daily,* in which she talks about monastic traditions and how they can apply to anyone's daily life. I highly recommend the book. But she said something there, and earlier in an interview with *U.S. Catholic,* about a Benedictine practice that goes all the way back to St. Benedict, the founder. The idea made a strong impression on me. The tradition is to treat everyday objects in our homes—our dishes, appliances, clothing—as though they were altar vessels used to carry the blessed Eucharist. Think about that the next time you load the dishwasher, leave your socks in the corner, or scatter your CDs all over the floor.

Practice

awareness and imagination. Vietnamese holy man Thich Nhat Hanh offered a way to activate the analogical imagination. Try it with your children. "The next time you have a tangerine to eat, please put it in the palm of your hand and look at it in a way that makes the tangerine real." He suggested that just two or three seconds of awareness can make a vast difference. He said you will begin to notice within that fruit a beautiful blossom, sunshine, earth, and rain. You will witness a tiny fruit forming and developing into the tangerine that sits in your hand. Such awareness opens your eyes to the common miracles that surround you.

Be mindful of

the people you are putting into your children's lives. Are your children in contact with their larger, extended family? Do your regular visitors include people whose lives speak of spiritual growth and interest?

Keep ethnic and religious

traditions alive. Are there practices you experienced when you were little that you have let lapse since you've been grown—such as special meals tied to feasts and seasons or decorations around the home? These traditions once spoke volumes to you, and they can speak to your children today.

Allow the light

of faith to shine in your life. The light of faith goes beyond religious practice. This light shines out of your belief that God loves you. Do you demonstrate this faith and the belief that God is present in the midst of your life and that the life you are living is indeed holy? That light will shine on your children and attract them as they learn and grow.

*Sacred objects become the
principle connection between the
divine and the lived experience of
ordinary family life.*

ROBERT WUTHNOW

CHAPTER FIVE

Objects, Spaces, and Rituals
Holiness That Lives Close to Home

From time to time, I'll ask people to name a sacred object in their home. I stress that the object doesn't have to be overtly religious, like a holy statue or a crucifix. You might want to stop a minute and answer the question for yourself right now. Whenever I ask this question, I get some interesting stories.

One woman identified a breadboard that had belonged to her mother as a sacred object in her home. It hangs in her kitchen, and she uses it on special occasions. Each knife groove in the well-worn wood speaks to her of her mother's love. It sets her memory awash with smells of the warm bread that her mother baked daily for the family through the years.

I've heard people cite a range of objects from an emerald necklace given on a twenty-fifth wedding anniversary to a beat-up golf putter that belonged to a favorite uncle to a set of tools handed down for generations.

The objects in our homes are silent witnesses to the sacred we have experienced in the ordinary. Though mute, they speak of the love that's been there, of the joy that was shared, of the sacrifices made and the tenderness shown. Sometimes we fail to see it at the time, as when kids take their home for granted. But when moving day comes, they see everything with new, more appreciative eyes. Think back to your own home during your growing-up years. I'm sure there are places and objects there that almost glow in your memory but that you hardly ever noticed in your day-to-day living.

KEEPIN' IT REAL

The reason I ask people to engage in this exercise is to get them thinking and talking about the sacred in a natural, rather than forced, way. Priest friends of mine tell me that they run into a forced and phony sense of holiness all the time. People they meet will be talking naturally, often with genuine depth and care and humor. But as soon as these people discover that my friends are priests, they change. They apologize for their previous conversation (although there was absolutely nothing wrong with what they were talking about). Then they strain their brains to think of supposedly "holy" topics, like "Where's the pope been lately?" or "Would you happen to know this third cousin of mine who once studied in the seminary?" or "What are the odds of Notre Dame's making it to the Rose Bowl?" This reaction reveals the split so many of us experience between what we perceive as holy and how we normally live.

But when people reflect on sacred objects from their home, they get in touch with something very real and elemental. They come to know what *sacred* means in a tangible way. They've experienced it. They've touched it. All of a sudden, the phony, pseudoreligious tone that can emerge when people talk about spiritual things gets stripped away. When people talk about what they find sacred in daily life, the reasons they put forth tend to be grounded in real life, honest language, and deep relationships. Thus, they are in the right frame of mind to think about spirituality that connects to real life. They can leave behind the spirituality talk that is mere fluff or that is alienating.

Being a parent gives you daily opportunities to experience life at sacred depths. Think of the parent holding the little teddy bear that belonged to the child who died too young. Imagine the dad who takes his coffee break using the "World's Greatest Dad" mug he got from the stepchild who had greeted him with such suspicion and hostility just years before. Think of the mom who straightens her son's room and always gives an extra bit of care to the speech trophy won by a boy who found the grace to overcome his terrifying shyness.

Our lives are filled with sacred objects. St. Benedict told his monks to treat all household items as if they were vessels of the altar. They are. They bear Christ to us just as surely as the paten and the chalice bear Christ to us on Sunday.

THE SACRED JIGSAW PUZZLE

Someone turned the tables and asked me to name a sacred object in my own home. I thought awhile, and an obvious answer came to mind. In our house, one sacred object is the circle puzzle. It's a round jigsaw puzzle we bought from the UNICEF catalog. In its center are stars and planets floating in outer space. In concentric bands around that are animals and landscapes from all around the globe. Ringing the whole puzzle are people in native dress, representatives from all the world's cultures, holding hands. I've always liked the symbolism of the puzzle: The world and its peoples are connected in a circle with no beginning and no end. No one can claim to be number one. We are all connected to one another, to our geographies, to the wildlife around us. And in the center are the heavens. That's all nice and good.

But what makes this puzzle *sacred* to me are the times we shared as a family putting the puzzle together. We bought the thing when our kids were little, and back then it took us hours to get all the pieces in place. When people use the vague phrase *quality time,* doing the puzzle together with my family is what I think of. The TV would be off; perhaps we put on a few albums of show tunes and popped some popcorn. We've spent hours gathered in our own family circle, puzzling over how to put all the pieces of the world in place.

A year ago, I came across the puzzle in the attic. We hadn't put it together for years. Our girls have busy social lives and are often on their way out the door as Kathleen and I are groggily heading to bed. But that night we all stayed home and did the puzzle again. I was surprised at how fast we could put it together. My girls have grown. They know their way around the world so much better now. The puzzle taught all of us important lessons about unity and cooperation, about trial and error, about geography and customs, and about fun.

Ours is a sacramental world—full of tangible signs showing us Christ and giving us grace. A big part of passing on a living faith to our children is to help them see their world, our shared home, as filled with objects that reveal God in all the divine manifestations. Then, when they go to church and the bread is held up and the wine is poured, they'll be accustomed to seeing miracles right before their very eyes.

Susan M. Bennett wrote about that connection between life and worship in the January 1997 *Liturgy 90.* She reflected on lessons she's learned while baking bread for her parish's eucharistic celebration. She has baked the bread weekly for years, and she invited her daughters to help (the youngest one of three is now her assistant). She talked about the value of this action, how it deepens her and her daughters' participation in the Eucharist. On her recipe for bread that fulfills the canonical requirements of the Latin rite of the Roman Catholic Church, she wrote:

> A final word about the recipe: Bread is a living thing. Baking bread is a living process. Each parish, each bread baker, needs to experiment with the recipe to discover how best to bake it. So in order to bake a worthy bread for the Eucharist, one must have practice baking other kinds of bread for other kinds of feasts. And in order to break and serve the bread of the Eucharist on Sunday worthily, one must have practice breaking and serving bread in a myriad of self-sacrificing ways every day of the week.

We need to practice Eucharist throughout the week if it's going to have any meaning for us on Sunday. We need to cultivate within our children as well as within ourselves a feel for the elements of liturgy: waiting in silence, listening, offering, uniting, sharing, receiving, opening to the Word of God. We need to develop an innate appreciation of how ordinary objects (like bread and wine) can take us to a deeper place inside ourselves. This is the place where the illusion of our separateness from God and one another falls away and we experience the truth that Jesus spoke: "I am the vine; you are the branches."

We cultivate this awareness and aptitude in our children by exposing them to it, that is, by filling our children's lives with rich symbols, stories, music, imagery, and as much self-sacrificing love as we can muster. A good first step is to increase our own awareness and sensitivity to such times, places, objects, and rituals. Here are a few ideas I've gleaned from my own experience and from writing a family-spirituality newsletter for parents.

SACRED TIME

There is something magical about time. It changes shape and feel with lightning speed. One minute you're bored, feeling as though time plods endlessly through knee-high muck. The next minute, time is racing, filled with excitement. Something new and interesting is happening every second. And perhaps the only thing that has changed is what's going on in your own mind.

Time is relative. A mother and a child both have the same amount of time between December 20 and Christmas morning. But the child feels that time is dragging and Christmas will never come, while Mom panics that time is flying by so fast that she'll never be able to get everything done by Christmas morning. And despite everything we try in this mortal life, we can neither capture time nor escape it.

"Now is the acceptable time," says the Lord. The acceptable time for what? To live. To be. To experience connection with a God who loves us and who fills this moment with divine life. Our lesson is to learn to be where we are and do what we're doing. That is why meditation is so helpful—and so difficult. In meditation, we try to simply be in the presence of God's overwhelming love. But as we first attempt it, we soon recognize that we rarely live in the present moment. We worry about how we're going to pay off the car loan, whether the furnace will last another winter. We worry about what Johnny's going to do for the science fair next month or whether Suzy will ever be friends again with Melissa. We feel twinges as memories of our various social blunders cruelly and endlessly replay themselves in the theater of our mind. We're everywhere but *here*.

One advantage of family life as a spiritual path is that it is constantly calling us to be in the present, to attend to *now, here, this*. Family life can be either a series of endless distractions or a continuing opportunity to be in the moment. We can respond to that challenge if we practice mindfulness— awareness of who we are, where we are, what we're doing— and are open to God's presence in the here and now.

There's a story about the Buddha that makes sense for any spiritual tradition. The Buddha was asked if he was a prophet.

"No, not a prophet," he replied.

"Are you then a god?"

"No, not a god."

"Are you a saint?"

"No, not a saint."

"Then what are you?"

"I'm awake."

Our aim is to be awake to a new reality beneath the reality that we're so used to perceiving. Once we awaken to the new reality, we understand that we have all that we need and all the time there is, for we are never separated from God's love. This awakening takes practice. We can achieve it one moment and lose it the next. That's OK. That's how life is for human beings. But as life unfolds within our family, we can practice mindfulness and awareness. We can pay attention and be alert to clues for that new reality, and we can be awake to see some of the miracles happen.

Taking action _4_

How your family can learn

to notice sacred time

Teach your children to start each day with prayers. A good prayer to teach them is a morning offering. I learned the following when growing up. A copy of this prayer was always on our bathroom mirror.

> O Jesus, through the Immaculate Heart of Mary, I offer you my prayers, works, joys, and sufferings of this day, for all the intentions of the Sacred Heart, in union with the holy Catholic Church throughout the world and the communion of saints.

Here's another prayer you can consider.

> Jesus, my brother, I thank you for the gift of today. I offer you all that I will do with this day: my working and my playing, my trials and my triumphs, my sorrows and my joys. They all belong to you. Help me to live in peace with my brothers and sisters here and around the world. Help me to grow ever

closer to you and to thank you for your love when evening comes. Amen.

Put a saint-of-the-day calendar on your breakfast table. You can buy a nice calendar with short entries about the saint whose feast is celebrated that day, or pick up a *Lives of the Saints* for families. Reading the passage of the day gives you the chance to teach your children important lessons about holy people whose example we can emulate, and it also conveys a sense that our days have meaning and worth.

Make Saturday night special. As the week segues from business-as-usual to the restful experience promised by observance of the Sabbath, mark this special time with your children by helping them switch gears. A friend told me, "I remember that Saturday night became special when we were called in from playing and bath time began. We each took our baths, got in our jammies, and either played a board game or watched an old-time movie as a family. It was the one night we were allowed to drink pop and eat popcorn. It seemed as if the week had suddenly changed, that time itself slowed and the outside noise abated and we had this special time all to ourselves as a family. And so when Sunday morning came, it seemed we were all in the frame of mind for going to church. Not that we always wanted to go, but it seemed to flow from the specialness of the night before."

You can prepare your family to get more out of church by shaping what goes on in your home during the hours beforehand. Your habits and traditions can signal a certain atmosphere by how they set this time of the week apart from what passes for normal. There's no one set formula. Find a routine that works for you; then be faithful to it.

Make birthdays special.
One of the saddest stories I ever heard was about the time my friend Kevin turned fifteen and ended up having to bake his own birthday cake. Everyone else was away or forgot. Celebrating a person's birth is a central way to convey a sense of time's sacredness. Life can get hectic. It's understandable that a parent might get overwhelmed by the demands of life and simply blow off the occasion of a child's birthday. Alternately, many parents get caught up in the competitiveness of "who is throwing the most fun and exciting party" so that the event becomes about enhancing their image rather than about expressing loving appreciation for the child who was born into their lives this day. Keep your eye on the prize. The point of celebrating is to convey how much you cherish this child, and straightforward and simple are usually better than elaborate, as expressed through "things."

Find a time each birthday to sit together with your child and share a special message just from you. It might be about the day he or she was born, about how much you were looking forward to having this child. Or you can mention one or more traits of this child that bring you joy. If you do that early in the day, I'll bet the rest of the day goes well, no matter how many wild kids show up for the party.

Celebrate

the night before the first day of school. Whenever there are passages from one season to another or from one style of living to another, it's wise to mark these times with an appropriate celebration. Some events deserve a party, others just a special time together. The night before school begins can be an anxious time, and you can help your children get in the right frame of mind by accompanying them during this transition.

One family I know sets aside the night before school begins as story night. Each person has to tell at least one story from the previous year about him- or herself or about the family. Some of the stories are hilarious. Some are quite poignant. But it's a chance to solidify connections and gather strength before beginning the adventure of a new school year. It gives everyone the chance to calm down and switch gears from

summertime ways of living. Starting school is a big deal, and taking steps like this will help your children know that they are not alone.

Celebrate ethnic holidays and feasts—even if it's not your ethnic group. My German mother-in-law always made shamrock pancakes for her children on St. Patrick's Day. Everyone in my neighborhood goes to the St. Joseph's table—even if we're not Italian or Polish. The growing number of Hispanics in the U.S. is enriching our culture with traditional feasts for Our Lady of Guadalupe, Our Lady of Charity, Los Posadas (a reenactment of Joseph and Mary searching Bethlehem for a place to stay), and myriad observances throughout the year. Light candles on the Feast of St. Lucy (December 13), patron of light and sight. Find out who the patron saint of your profession or nation of origin is and celebrate that

feast day. There are countless ways to spice up the calendar year with special celebrations. They convey without words that all the days are special. The whole year is bathed in holiness.

Make more of your time in
the car together. These days, parents may see more of their children in the car than in the home. Do yourself and your children a favor and abstain from asking questions in the car. The kind of questions I mean are, "When will you be home?" "Did you do your homework?" "Did you remember to bring that form that needed to be filled out?" Instead, sit and listen. Your children may not talk to you—especially if they're with their friends. But you'll learn a lot anyway. Pretend you're the disinterested chauffeur, and you'll hear an earful.

But if you're alone with your children, let them take the initiative. You can ask something leading: "Have you got any questions about life that are on your mind?" or "Is there something you'd like to tell me if I promised not to yell?" Then sit back and listen. Your listening attitude can draw your children out. Children need and want to control the flow of information about themselves. We all do. The more listening you do, the more you'll find out, and the closer you'll become.

Once in a while, why not flip off the radio and sing together in the car? Your children may groan, but as time goes on they might come to enjoy it. Sing show tunes, popular songs, camp songs, and hymns from church on Sunday. This is guaranteed to make a trip to the orthodontist out of the ordinary.

And when two or more are gathered, at any minute, Christ just might break in.

SACRED OBJECTS AND PLACES

From earliest civilization, human beings have marked off certain places as sacred. The Pyramids, ancient ruins, shrines, and cathedrals hold special places in our psyche. Pilgrims travel to the Holy Land to walk where Jesus walked, see where he was born, press their palms to olive trees that may have been alive when he prayed in the garden, and find the holy sepulchre where he lay buried.

Walk back to your old neighborhood; it transports you to a different time and place and reality. We have sacred places in our homes today. Is it the porch swing where the family sits on summer evenings, quieting down from the events of the day and settling in to a unity that speaks of God's love? Is it the dining-room table where you gather for holidays and special occasions, where Grandma and Grandpa sit as honored guests and the room is ringed with aunts and uncles, cousins, and shirttail relatives who find family with you?

In our house, one sacred place is our gold chair. It's worn and ragged, but we'll never get rid of it. Kathleen and I bought the chair when we were first married and didn't have a nickel to our names. If wise money management were the only criteria for purchasing furniture, we had no business buying it. But it was an investment in our life as a family; the chair became a sort of anchor for us, tying us solidly to our values because of what the chair came to mean to us.

It was the chair we brought our babies home to, the place they were fed, rocked, held, whispered to, comforted, and played with. We held not only our own babies but also other babies whom we were watching or welcoming as visitors to our home. It became the chair in which we seated the honored guest. And during the years we met with a faith-sharing group from the parish, it took on a special character.

After the group had been meeting for a number of months, someone commented that it seemed as though whoever sat in the gold chair was the one who ended up pouring his or her guts out to the group. It became a running joke. Sometimes, as the guests arrived, one of the group would make a beeline for the chair, saying something like "I've had a hellish week. It's my turn in the chair." The chair came to symbolize the group at its best. In its comforting arms, people felt free enough to share their worries, agonies, and tales of woe, knowing that they would be received kindly, with compassion, faith, hope, and love.

It takes a sense of the sacred to counter today's obsession with disposing of everything at the first sign of wear or the first inkling that buying a newer product could give us a buzz.

Taking action 5

How to increase your family's sense of the sacred

Adorn the house with objects reflecting your beliefs and values—both overtly religious and inherently so. If strangers walked into your home, would they know that you are a follower of Jesus? Would they know what your values are? Make it a point to select artwork and decorations that convey your beliefs and values. These objects speak volumes to your children, and these objects retain that power throughout the children's lives.

Help your children select their own religious symbol for their room. It can be a statue of their patron saint, a banner or poster with an uplifting message, a statue of St. Francis of Assisi, or a copy of the wonderful prayer attributed to him. Each child should have his or her own age-appropriate copy of the Bible. Jesus as the Good Shepherd is a favorite of younger kids. Get hold of a good religious-art catalog or visit a religious-goods store with each child and make a selection or two just for him or her. Arnold Schwarzenegger isn't the only larger-than-life hero who belongs on your children's walls.

Create a quiet area or room in your house, a space where there is no TV noise or distraction. This area can be a place the kids do their homework, a spot where you can have a quiet and serious conversation or just daydream. With all the noise of modern life, a place of relative quiet can indeed be sacred.

Let your refrigerator door preach your values. Put up pictures of godchildren, pictures of family friends, prayer cards commemorating relatives who have died, photos of children you sponsor through foreign-relief services, snippets of text that you find inspiring, a motto you want to live by, a favorite family prayer. Everything you put up on your refrigerator door also takes a spot in your children's subconscious. Use that space wisely.

Broaden the sense of family.

We once ordered a calendar from UNICEF that featured stunning photos of children from around the world. Each month our children got to meet through those photos children from another culture. We'd talk about the country, what it was like, what we knew of its culture and challenges. I think our children developed a sense of the brotherhood and sisterhood of all the peoples of the world. Often our children don't have an opportunity to meet people of other cultures directly.

This is one way to raise them with a sense of the world's diverse cultures.

Your children glimpse (in some cases, come to know well) other cultures when you make a point to invite people of different cultures and ethnic groups into your home. One of the great scandals of our age is the divisiveness between peoples. You can be part of the solution or part of the problem. Isolation is a big part of the problem. Our children will be faced with mounting challenges to find a way to live with many cultures in an increasingly small world. They will fare much better if they're introduced early on to the humanity of all people.

SACRED RITUALS

Don't think that rituals need to be holy, formal, or serious. They may have become major family traditions or have simply achieved the status of "the way we do things." A ritual can be as simple as looking out the same window every morning and saying hello to the birds gathered at the bird feeder or as involved as putting on a major feast every Thanksgiving. They may even seem mundane, but rituals are the actions and habits we return to that give shape, form, and meaning to our lives.

One of the values of rituals is that they can call us back when we're on the verge of getting lost. A friend told me he had been having trouble with his preteen daughter. They had been very close in previous years, but lately she seemed to find fault with everything he said, and she rarely found time to spend with him and the rest of the family. He was worried that she was drifting away and that he'd lose her. He especially missed the times when everyone else was out of the house and they'd make popcorn and watch the *Three Stooges* together. He laughed as he remembered how they would take turns mimicking Curly's "Nyuk, nyuk, nyuk."

One rainy day he noticed in the TV listings that there was going to be a *Three Stooges* film festival all day on one of the UHF channels. He was nervous, but he took a chance. He called up the stairs to her room and told her about the film festival. It took some courage, but he added, "I'd really love for the two of us to spend some time together again, honey."

What felt like a horribly long pause ensued. Then he heard her voice, now so mature, asking, "So, you gonna make the popcorn or should I?" Spending that afternoon on the couch watching three goofs poke each other in the eyes carried dad and daughter through some long, difficult adolescent days to come.

Author and family-faith expert Kathleen O'Connell-Chesto told the editors of *U.S. Catholic* about recent research on the value of ritual.

> The Wolins, a husband and wife team from George Washington University, did a study on alcoholic families, particularly those families that succeeded in not handing alcoholism on to the third generation. The one thing they found that the "successful" families all had in common was rituals—they called them ritual protected families. The Wolins suggest that rituals made the families secure and gave them a sense of identity and belonging.

Which rituals in particular? "They specifically mentioned bedtime, mealtime, and holiday rituals," said O'Connell-Chesto.

I've experienced how simple rituals can keep a family connected. My parents have a cottage on a small lake in Michigan. We love to go up there, and we usually spend a week each summer. Years ago, when the kids were younger and we were playing in the sand in the shallow water near the shore, the kids were getting bored. So we invented a game. It's a simple game that kids from preschool on up can play. One person thinks of a television sitcom and describes the main characters and their family relationships. For example: "There's a dad and a mom, two older sisters, a son, and two younger sisters." If necessary, you give more clues. (The answer to this one? *The Cosby Show,* original version.) Whoever guesses first gets to set forth the next puzzle.

Sure enough, last summer we were way out, floating in the middle of the lake on rafts and inner tubes, and without any kind of announcement, we picked up the game where we left off the summer before—and everyone joined in without a hitch. We only play this game up at the lake; and every time we're there we play it. It's *our* game, special to us and the guests who've joined us at the lake. Is it a goofy game? Yes. But is it sacred? Only if family connection is sacred. To answer that question I need only think of the hours in golden sunlight spent with daughters who were going through the ups and downs of adolescence, finding their way in life. I thought of how, by playing the game we had played years ago, we were able to return to a place where we were sure we'd find one another. Yes, it's sacred.

Taking action 6

How to build on the rituals you already have

Make more out of Advent. Get an Advent wreath, light the candles in order, and sing a hymn at dinner every night. This is a powerful practice. In the darkness of December, you begin a ritual wherein you darken your home, light one candle, and join your voices in song: "O come, O come, Emmanuel, and ransom captive Israel, that mourns in lonely exile here until the Son of God appear." Each week, you light an additional candle, and the light around your table grows.

Get an Advent calendar so that your children can focus on the preparation for Jesus' coming during the days before Christmas. These are available (many of them quite inexpensive) in most card shops or drugstore chains, as well as in religious bookshops. The opening of one door a day builds anticipation and the sense that life is a search for mystery and that, in the words of author Mary Jo Pedersen, "there's more to life than meets the eye."

Put your children in charge of the manger scene. If they bicker over this, buy one for each child. Scholars say that St. Francis of Assisi reevangelized Europe with the introduction of the manger scene as a worship aid and teaching tool. It can work on your children too. (You won't have to worry that these action figures are filling your children's heads with violent or sexist messages.)

You can take similar steps for other seasons, such as Lent, Easter, and Thanksgiving, enriching the whole year and reinforcing the sense that faith makes more of our days.

Give each child a great send-off. Make it a family habit to bless your children in their comings and goings. This is a ritual in most Hispanic homes. A quick tracing of the sign of the cross on the forehead as your child leaves for school or for play conveys your deepest hopes that he or she will remain safely in the sight of God all day.

And there's evidence that such greetings serve to increase family closeness and satisfaction. Writing in *Context,* his newsletter on religion and culture, church historian Martin E. Marty reported on a study that asked what habits improved the intimacy of married couples. "Among all the variables in the habits of the couples studied, one ritual of intimacy stood out," wrote Rev. Paul Bosch. "Did the couple embrace and kiss at the door in the morning before going their separate ways to work, or did they not?" The couples who kissed reported having happier, longer, and more fulfilling marriages than those couples who did not.

Not surprising, perhaps. As Bosch added, "Whatever you do repeatedly, over and over again, has the power to shape you." But the real surprise was that it didn't seem to matter whether or not the couples meant it!

"Just a perfunctory peck on the cheek seemed to be enough—enough to make a difference in the quality of the relationship."

That's something to mull over when your kids say they don't want to go to church because they get nothing out of it. Or when they don't want to hold hands when you pray grace before meals, or they try to sneak out of the house without your giving them a quick blessing. The action itself shapes us and improves the quality of our relationship.

The gestures themselves have power in them. Make the effort, and the rituals of your life will shape you, change you, elevate you. And they will shape your children as well.

Say good-night to your sweet prince and princess. Bedtime rituals are of the utmost importance in maintaining a healthy relationship with your children. Saying "I love you" before bedtime, tucking the young child in, or spending just a moment in contact with the older child—all are powerful rituals that make an enormous difference in the child's sense of well-being.

It's especially important as the child grows up to replace old bedtime rituals with new ones. Your child may not want you to read *Scruffy the Tugboat* anymore, but a minute spent saying, "As the day ends, I always thank God I get to be your dad [or your mom]" is an age-appropriate way to smooth the transition from waking to sleeping, from day into darkness of night. Use your imagination and your knowledge of each particular child to arrive at a bedtime routine that is reassuring and connecting.

Eat dinner with your children. There's perhaps no more powerful ritual in the development of your children's spiritual capacity than the family meal. "How do we teach the nature of the Eucharist as a meal to families who never eat together?" asked Father Alfred Ciferni, O. Praem. It's as simple as this: Commit to sit down and eat a meal together at least five times a week. There may be days when schedules conflict, but what can be more important in your children's lives than arming them with the sense that they have a place in this world?

Rituals aren't magic, and sacred objects aren't an end in themselves. Those who get attuned to symbols of daily life know that these rituals and objects represent something real: the depth of one person's love for another, a sense of community, the presence of God. They function as channels of grace. The more we and our children are attuned to them, the more awake we will be to God's life and love all around us.

A Closer Look

The Amazing Power of Rituals

I got a lesson on the power of rituals at a recent Holy Thursday Mass. After our pastor washed the feet of twelve parishioners of various ages, the rest of the congregation was called to the altar. The pastor and associates were to wash each parishioner's hands in aromatic water laced with the perfume used in the baptismal oils. The church was packed, and slowly people milled forward. When you got to the front, you dipped your hands in a deep porcelain bowl filled with cool water. The priest bathed your hands and wished you peace. After your hands were washed, you turned to the person in line ahead of you, who took a fluffy towel and dried your hands. You then took the towel and waited to dry the hands of the person who came after you.

The kindness that people show—a man drying the arthritic hands of his wife so tenderly, so tenderly—is enough to turn stony hearts to hearts of flesh. A mother dries her daughter's tiny hands; that tiny daughter earnestly dries her father's beefy, mechanic's hands. As I get closer, I feel bathed in light, the light of God's love. I find myself surprised at the

95

long procession of people willing to be vulnerable like this, to open their lives, even in a small way, to one another. The choir alternates songs in English and Spanish; we're all trying to find ways to get along. Sometimes it goes well, but other times we misunderstand and hurt one another. That's nothing new in parishes. But in this line I see longtime pillars of the church drying the hands of newcomers who say their prayers in an alien tongue. And I see recent immigrants drying the hands of women whose faces—almost hardened into permanent scowls—now soften and who utter thank you with their lips and their eyes.

This is not a perfunctory "going through the motions." Even if it starts out that way, it won't remain so for long. Fear is the first casualty, and it soon departs. Wariness falls away. The music invites us and unites us. Eyes meet eyes; hands touch hands. For a moment we lay down our weary burdens and recognize our common humanity. The water washes away not only the dirt but also the edginess, the suspicion, the distance between us.

A stumbling block for many people seems to be the inability to imagine that these mundane actions—drying the hands of another, singing and praying in the language of the stranger, smiling with warmth and welcome—can be holy. The same is true with our daily actions in the family. People suspect that if what goes on in their homes is so sacred, then it's not much of a God they're dealing with. It diminishes their sense of holy. They just can't see it.

But with the right eyes to see, everyday activities become revelations. Remember the parable where the people asked, "When did we see you hungry, Lord? When did we see you thirsty?"

Jesus replied, "Whenever you fed the hungry or gave drink to the thirsty, you did that to me." And what parent has not fed the hungry, clothed the naked, given drink to the thirsty? What mom or dad has not cared for the sick and even visited the one in prison—sometimes truly in jail, sometimes caught up in the prison of fear, worry, shyness, being bullied by classmates, and so on. When did we see you, Lord?

"Whenever you did these things for the least of your brothers and sisters, you did it for me." Oh, then. Yeah, then.

And the point is not just to do difficult things in order to rack up points on the heavenly scoreboard. Within these activities themselves, we find the experience of feeding Jesus (which is the great irony because it is he who was born in a food trough to be food for the world and he who gives his own self to us in the Eucharist), of clothing Jesus, of encountering Jesus.

This is a mystery; this is a paradox. More on that in the next chapter.

Peace I leave with you;
my peace I give to you.
I do not give to you
as the world gives.

JESUS CHRIST (JOHN 14:27)

CHAPTER SIX

Paradise and Paradox

Helping Kids Grasp Faith Concepts

I was about eleven when I first heard the beautiful hymn at the conclusion of the funeral rite: "May the angels lead you into paradise; may the martyrs come to welcome you and take you to the holy city." As an altar boy facing the grim duty of tending to the funeral rite, I was consoled by the idea of an honor guard of angels escorting the dearly departed on his or her way to heaven.

I borrowed (and adapted) the phrase to introduce this chapter on paradox as part of the spiritual path. I believe this is an area of spiritual development where we need to be led rather than boldly charge ahead under our own steam.

When our children master new material in math, history, or geography, we say that they've grasped the concept. But in the world of spiritual development, grasping is the opposite of what you want to have happen. In fact, the process of growing in the Spirit is more about openness than closure, more about *being* grasped than about grasping. If you want your kids to develop a spiritual life, it will be good to give them an appetite for mystery and paradox.

Jesus spent a lot of time and energy trying to get his followers to see the deeper reality beneath life's surface. He did this by telling stories in which the obvious conclusion got turned on its head: The first becomes last, and the last is welcomed as first. The hated foreigner turns out to be the true neighbor. The high and mighty are refused entrance to the feast, but the poor and the outcast are welcomed gladly. The grain of wheat must die before it can bear fruit.

In Jesus' view, in order to make any real spiritual progress you need to embrace the strange logic of paradox. You need to be willing and able to accept mystery without trying to force a black-and-white answer to emerge. You need to remain open to the possibility of a new wisdom. Trying to force a black-and-white answer in the face of paradox can lead to fundamentalism and/or legalism. The need for certainty can lead us to put God in a box (or nail Jesus to a cross).

Jesus' message naturally had more appeal for the outcast and downtrodden than for the Goody Two-shoes of his day. Those on top of the heap weren't eager to hear the truth that we need to surrender in order to gain victory. Or that it is in acknowledging our weakness that we become fortified with God's strength.

With mere human vision, what you see is what you get. There's a certain obvious logic to it. If you want to be financially successful, you better go accumulate as much money as you can. But in the world of the Spirit, a different logic pertains. "He who would be first among you, should be last." In the human world, the one with authority over others rightly takes on the trappings of power. In the world of the Spirit, Jesus modeled another approach for leaders. He got down on his knees and washed his followers' feet, saying, "This is how you serve one another."

The list of paradoxes in the gospel is sizable. For example:

- The first shall be last, and the last shall be first.
- We must surrender in order to find victory.
- Blessed are those who mourn (all the Beatitudes are paradoxes).
- Unless a grain of wheat falls to the ground, it shall not bear fruit.
- In order to gain mature happiness, we must become like little children.
- To find ourselves, we should forget ourselves.
- We gain personal happiness by tending to the well-being of others.
- Our weaknesses can be a source of greater strength.
- It is by dying that we are born to eternal life.

In the world of the Spirit, paradox is the passageway to growth. Paradox is not so much something you're taught as something you're introduced to. Like the finer skills of working with wood or preparing a flaky piecrust, living with paradox is not a skill to be learned by rote. We learn to live with paradox as though we were apprentices absorbing lessons.

If our children don't pick up a sense of the paradoxical, all they'll know is what's on the surface of life. They'll miss the depth and the peace that Jesus gives and, at best, experience only the elusive ease that the world promises.

LENT IS A TIME TO CHECK YOUR VISION

You'll find a number of great opportunities to initiate your children into the world of paradox and spiritual awareness throughout the year. Perhaps one of the most powerful and obvious is Lent, which is a time designed for sitting with paradox. In Lent we practice fasting, a chance to experience an emptiness that can show us how filled we are. We give up certain habits and practices—thereby curtailing our freedom—so that we can experience the freedom of seeing new truths about our lives. We celebrate and reenact terrible events during the days of Holy Week, events that we label the Good News.

Taking action 7

How to involve your children during Lent

Practice the traditions of fasting, prayer, and giving to the poor. These are Christian traditions but are also important components of other world religions. You can encourage your children to give up a favorite snack or TV show and pay attention to their feelings in its absence. They may discover anxiousness, hunger, or self-centeredness. Or they may experience new energy and curiosity about other projects and adventures. Coming to such an awareness is a valuable spiritual experience.

Encourage your children to pray for someone who has hurt them. This is a way to introduce your children to the concept of Christian forgiveness. Don't demand or expect that your children will like the offender. But Jesus tells us to do good to those who hurt us.

Select a worthy charity or mission opportunity that you will donate to as a family during Lent. Some families put a small collection bowl on the kitchen table, and at dinnertime family members can contribute to the cause. Holding a family discussion on where to give the money will open your children's eyes to the needs of others in the world and their responsibility to act in charity and justice for the good of others.

Have your children commit a secret act of kindness for someone who irritates them. This deed shouldn't be done with manipulation or with the expectation of reward or recognition. Another practice that I try to remember and that I've shared with my daughters is to bow inwardly upon meeting other people. You don't have to do anything overt; just simply make an interior bow of respect. This is particularly helpful when going into a difficult situation or meeting someone for the first time, it takes the concentration off of fear and replaces it with recognition that every person is a child of God.

Encourage

your children to read spiritual biographies. Populate your children's imagination with stories that run contrary to the normal success story. Introduce your children via books and videos to people who made a choice to live their life with faith. Catholics have the tradition of *Lives of the Saints,* which is packed with ordinary people who led extraordinary lives. But every religious tradition continues to tell the stories of its heroes, and most religious presses offer a line of books for children of various ages. Consult a salesperson at your local religious bookstore for guidance.

Participate with

your children in your local church's Lenten services. For instance, Ash Wednesday reminds us of the paradox that we are mere dust but are also "a little lower than the angels." We are dust, yet God's Son became flesh and died for us. Confronting our limits and our mortality, as Ash Wednesday invites us to do, introduces us to the deep mystery that awaits within us: "Who am I? Who made me? What is my destiny?"

Invite your children

to examine their consciences. It's important to have a balanced sense of our own sinfulness as well as the all-encompassing mercy of God. In the Catholic tradition, many parishes hold Lenten reconciliation services that help address two modern villains: the sense that I can never be worthy and the contrary sense that I am quite fine on my own, thank you very much. The first approach tells us that we must struggle and struggle before we can ever hope to earn God's love. The other approach tells us that we don't really need God's love. Both are wrong. An honest sense of contrition is the prelude to mercy. It turns out that we do need God's love and that God's love is always available if we will just stop playing God ourselves. Rituals such as lighting a candle, reading appropriate passages from Scripture, and saying the Our Father together can signify remorse as well as the light of God's love, present to us always.

Make Holy Week special. Take

advantage of the traditions of your denomination for celebrating Holy Week. Take steps to indicate that this is not life as usual, but a special time set apart. Do that through what you eat, what you do in the evenings, what you talk about, and what you do upon waking and going to sleep. For example, you might set aside an

evening to read the Gospel accounts of Jesus' passion and death. Encourage your local church to try to involve younger people in any Holy Week ceremonies, and prepare your children for such participation by explaining what the symbols and readings mean to you.

If you know of Easter and Holy Week traditions from your ethnic heritage, introduce them to your children. Many families decorate eggs—symbols of the Resurrection— or put together Easter baskets that will be blessed at church. Many churches have services that are filled with meaningful symbols—like light shining forth in the darkness that cannot overcome it—and those rituals speak volumes directly to your child's heart. The story of Jesus' suffering and death are at the heart of Christian faith. They are at the heart of our very existence and meaning. It's easy to be too busy or too distracted to attend to these rites and lessons. But we deprive our children of life and meaning when we do so.

ORDINARY TIME IS SPECIAL TOO

Daily life offers many opportunities to introduce children to the paradoxical nature of our faith. Think of the times your child struggles with new concepts in school. The truth is that we can finally learn when we admit what we don't know. Think also of the times your child feels the desire to force another child's friendship or loyalty. The truth is that it's only when we stop trying to possess the other person that we can truly enjoy friendship. Likewise, it's only when we admit our need that we can be filled. And we come to fullness only when we're willing to experience our emptiness.

These are tough lessons, ones that don't come in a flash. It takes grace to see the logic of the spiritual laws, which so often differ from the physical laws that seem obvious. We want what we can see and smell and taste and touch. It takes spiritual maturity to trust that there is much more to be attained by letting go.

The church is not a community of the already converted. It's a community where conversion happens.

Anonymous

Here's a story to ponder about the difference between grasping and attaining. A man who loved Ireland as much as he loved life itself died clutching a piece of sod from his beloved country. As he approached the gates of heaven he was told he could only enter with empty hands. He agonized over letting go of this tie to his homeland, but finally he unclenched his fist. The gates of heaven opened, and behold, before him lay all of Ireland.

A Closer Look

Whatever Happened to Awe?

I work in downtown Chicago and traipse across "the Loop" every morning. Too often I make the trip with my head down and my mind filled with worries about the day to come. One gray day shortly after Thanksgiving, I was about to cross State Street, "that great street," when a bus pulled in front of me and I had to wait. I was annoyed. I was in a hurry. I had important things to do.

Off the bus came a mom and her young son. He was about five but had poise and attitude beyond his years. Stepping down from the bus, he stood on the curb with his hands on his hips. He looked left. He looked right. He looked all up and down the street. "Whoa!" he cried, to the world in general. "Who did all *that?*" And for the first time that season, I looked up and down and all around at the wondrous Christmas decorations on the storefronts and the lampposts and the newly planted trees. I smiled at the boy and said, "Thanks, I needed that."

I wish I had more awe in my life. I think Jesus wishes I did too. I used to experience awe more frequently when I was a kid, and when I was new at my job, and when I was taking the train downtown for the first hundred or so times, and when I was able to take my time doing chores in my garden or would stop in the middle of shoveling snow and simply let flakes fall stingingly on my cheeks. I remember feeling awe while standing on a ridge looking out at acres and acres of uninterrupted cornfields in central Illinois on a warm July day. I felt awe when my two daughters were born and when the waters of baptism flowed over their foreheads and, years later, when their faces lit up in candlelight at an Easter vigil.

Whatever happened to awe? Well, I checked a book of main themes of the Bible (*Harper's Topical Concordance*) and discovered that *awe* comes right after *awareness*. It seems that awe follows awareness in life as well. I suspect that I will always experience a shortage of awe if I'm simply not paying attention.

I think it can be hard for Americans to remain awake and aware on a daily basis. We have so many inducements and opportunities to avoid truly being present in our own lives. How often do you turn on the TV just for background noise, to mask the silence? How often do you eat and not taste, read and not absorb, touch and not feel? Have you driven by golden sunsets and had your mind on other things? Have you sat through a sermon and not heard a word—not heard *the* Word?

The problem is not that there are too few awesome events, inventions, sights, sounds, and experiences in our world. Quite the opposite. Where people once were amazed at silent moving pictures and then marveled at talkies, today's teenagers expect 360-degree screens, surround sound, and multimillion-dollar special effects—and still walk out bored. People easily travel to distant lands or have them brought into their homes via TV and movies. Megamalls offer hundreds of stores and millions of items of merchandise (though maddeningly not that one power drill or style of purse you've been seeking for years) and come equipped with waterfalls, ice rinks, and cash machines. In fact, there may be so many remarkable occurrences available to us that we're suffering a kind of inflation of expectation. It takes more "bang" to even raise an eyebrow.

I know that after a day of too many messages, too much stimulation, and too much diversion, I feel like the child at Christmas who sits amid a pile of torn wrapping paper and strewn packages feeling somehow empty and deprived. What's missing? Certainly not more *things.* What's missing is the nourishing food of God's presence. It's my quiet awareness of God's presence that produces awe.

The remedy to this modern dilemma seems to be a kind of renunciation. Turn off the noise so that you can hear. Stop the flashing lights so that you can see. Stop wolfing down food so that you can taste. Stop rushing so that you can get somewhere in your spiritual life. "Be still, and know that I am God!"

When was the last time you experienced awe? What made that event different from your daily routine? I suspect it came because you were paying attention. And you may have been paying attention because you had gotten out of that routine.

Look at Moses. He encountered the burning bush only after he had led his flocks (or did they lead him?) to the "west side of the wilderness." That means he traveled through some unknown wildlands and came to an unfamiliar, even frightening, place. When you travel "west of the wilderness," you can be certain that something new is going to happen to you. Something astounding happened for Moses, and it can for you. Dare to step out of your routine, and you may experience a new awareness of what's true every day, all day: You are being held in the palm of God's hand.

When you cultivate awe by paying more attention, you will, in time, come to realize that God is watching you with love. I once heard a man describe his profound prayer life this way: "I look at the good God, and the good God looks at me." That's awesome!

Taking action 8

How to develop your family's sense of awe

Take off your shoes.

Before Moses could approach the burning bush, he was admonished to take off his shoes. By doing so, he took on an attitude of respect. He also became more vulnerable and could feel the earth beneath his feet. While you needn't literally take off your shoes, you can signal your respect for God by getting down on your knees, praying with open hands, or going to church services early and sitting in silence.

Add some silence to your

life. Write daily in a journal if that appeals to you. In the quiet time, let go of your nagging worries and fears. Visualize yourself dropping them in God's lap. Let the silence restore your ability to appreciate the goodness of God's bounty.

Follow a child around.

Little children aren't as jaded as most adults. When you're with a small child, don't spend your time shushing and silencing. Rather, observe how delighted this child can be with the world. Go to the zoo, a park, or a museum and watch that child's face and learn to feel awe once again.

Suspend

your disbelief. Too often we feel that the direct experience of God's love happened in the old days and to special people. These lowered expectations limit your ability to feel wonder and awe. Start the day by saying, "If I did believe that God could touch my life in special ways today, how would I live?" Then act as if that, in fact, is true.

Stop and watch your child sleep. Doing this always overwhelmed me with joy when my girls were tiny babies, and as they grew, and even today. Our daily patterns and routines can be so powerful that when the girls are awake we're already dragged into issues of "Did you do your homework?" "Do you have your keys?" "Why do you always leave a mess?" Watching them sleep is a chance to see them as God sees us—with tenderness and kindness and hope for their best interests that just bubble up uninterrupted.

Make time to take time. How likely is it that your schedule includes an entry such as "15 minutes, sit and watch the sun shine through the water sprinkler" or "20 minutes, watch bird build nest in neighbor's tree" or "8 minutes, come across

Puccini's *Madama Butterfly* on classical music station, sit on stairs, and marvel." We schedule our work, but how often do we set aside time for living and loving? Work is good. Work is important. Work is an essential part of our spiritual path. But in a string of busy days, won't your life veer steadily out of balance if work is all you do? As the adult in the situation, you're the only one who will intervene on your own behalf. Whatever way you schedule your time, make sure to schedule time to pay more attention to life's little gifts.

Pay attention,

please! How often do we tell our children to pay attention? When they traipse across a clean floor with muddy boots, when they reach for the mustard and knock over the milk, when the doorbell rings and they sit staring blankly at a video screen, we're likely to say, "Won't you please pay attention!"

Get out of your routine.

Eat in the dining room if you normally eat in the kitchen. Instead of driving to church on Sunday, walk. Turn off the TV and listen to an offbeat radio show.

Get in touch with

nature. Nature is another place to come to know the pattern of dying and rising. Go camping, take nature walks, or do some gardening.

I don't expect to encounter burning bushes in my life, but I can watch maples turn to flame each autumn and daffodils come back to life each spring. If I don't distract myself, I can admit that I am a sinner who has been redeemed. That's a miracle! Miracles are happening around me if only I choose to be aware. If I open my eyes and my heart, I will discover what happened to awe.

*The kingdom of God
is like a healthy family
and is founded on love.*

BISHOP MICHAEL PFEIFER, O.M.I.

CHAPTER SEVEN

The Intentional Family
True Parenthood Is a Spiritual Path

Can you experience a kind of enlightenment while cleaning the bathroom? I believe so. It happened to me. One day while scouring a bathtub, I saw my life in a whole new light.

It was on a Saturday years ago. I was scrubbing and daydreaming when a new thought drifted into my head. It was as though a light went on. All of a sudden I somehow knew that scrubbing this tub was a holy work. In fact, my whole life as a husband, father, and extended family member took on a sacramental glow. I looked at the soap scum swirling down the drain and realized that at this very moment I was responding to an invitation to live with new eyes. I was hearing my calling.

As I recall, that day we were busy getting the house ready for company. We were having family members over for a birthday party, and I made a startling connection. I came to see the preparations we were making—cooking, cleaning, dragging chairs up from the basement, and setting the table—as a sacred activity. At first I wanted to say that these preparations were like preparing the altar for the Eucharist. But that seemed backward. It was more accurate to say that I finally saw that preparing the altar for the Eucharist was exactly like these homely activities—the cooking, cleaning, lugging—done in loving anticipation of communion with those who would soon arrive at our doorstep.

Religious ritual—which often seemed a little divorced from real life, something that existed a bit above me and my life—came into clearer focus. The plainness of taking bread and wine and sharing it became obvious. It's not as though magic were imposed on mundane activities; rather, the mystery was inherent in these activities and what they could render: depth, meaning, connection, and love.

I could imagine Jesus sitting on the edge of the tub saying, "You say you want to get close to me. Don't you realize how close I *already* am to you? Rigorously going through the motions of spending hours on your knees reciting prayers, as if in some endurance contest, is not going to achieve what you want. But when you're down on your knees scrubbing the floor, know that I am there. And I am there when you watch cartoons on Saturday morning with your daughters and when you strive to argue fairly with your wife as well as when you hold each other in reconciliation. And I am close to you when the whole clan gathers around a table of food prepared with love." That was a new and exciting way to look at my life.

Exciting though it was, this revelation didn't knock me off my horse or even make me slip in the tub. After all, we had company coming in a few hours, and I had no time to sit and ponder the eternal verities. But that was the beginning of a slow but steady change in my perception whereby I have come to see family life and parenting in a new and more accurate light. I see that the mundane actions of our days are revelatory—they reveal the sacred nature of our lives, our relationships, our living constantly in the embrace of God's love.

This perception leads to my conviction that *family life can be a spiritual path.* Typically when people think of a spiritual path, they think of renouncing family life for monastic life or life as a member of a religious order or congregation. But the activities of family life well lived are every bit as spiritually valuable as Benedict's rule or the monastery's routine. It's not the location or the situation that makes life holy; it's the openness we bring to it. And we don't have to impose a grand silence or put the kids in cloister (as much as we might want to some days!) or eschew family fun or intimacy to achieve it. Quite the contrary. We meet God *in* the family fun, *in* the intimacy, *in* the little bit of heaven on earth that can be our families when we cherish one another, welcome the stranger, support one another, plumb our deepest longings, and recognize God in our daily joys and tears as well as in the breaking of the bread at the family table.

BASIC TRAINING

Basic training is one way to view family life. Often, in the past, people thought of the family in hierarchical terms, with the parents (usually Dad) in the lead power role, and the kids in a subordinate role. The parents had the information; the kids learned from the parents. The relationship was one of distance, direction, and control.

In this mode, religious education was a matter of the parents announcing, "This is what you should believe, and this is how you ought to behave." The theme song for this style was "Onward, Christian Soldiers." In practice, this military-style approach to faith inducement was often softened by experience and the give-and-take of family life. But the underlying attitude was that faith was a matter of instruction. And much of the responsibility for the child's faith development was handed over to the Sunday school or parish, where the children were drilled in their catechism as you would drill a military unit. Adherence was just assumed.

But when parenting itself is seen as a spiritual path, the rules change. Surely one duty that parents have is to do what they can to pass faith on to their children. But taken from a spiritual point of view, the question for the parent becomes, "Where are *you* when you take on this task?" When I say, "*Where* are you?" I mean, "Where are you spiritually?" Are you acting out of power and coercion? Are you acting out of fear? Are you acting out of a confused or even hypocritical situation? Are you acting out of your own spiritual center?

For example, a father may be acting out of vanity when trying to get all his children to attend church regularly. He does business with the public and likes to be seen surrounded by well-scrubbed faces as he sits in a prominent place in church. I'm sure I won't surprise you if I tell you that this approach has little spiritual value other than as a stumbling block for your children to face and overcome.

Or consider a mother who pushes her daughter into a religious youth group, figuring the odds of her running into a "nice" boy are better than if she goes to the regular youth hangouts. This approach is not high on the spiritual hit parade either. That's not to say that these motives and actions are all that bad. We're human, and our motives are typically mixed. But the first question we're asked when we hope to treat being a parent as a spiritual path is, "Where are you coming from? What's your motivation?"

REALLY SIMPLE OR SIMPLY REAL

So the expectations change when we head out on the spiritual path of raising our kids in faith. The hope is that, more and more over time, *where* we are at is in the heart of God. Since God is love, we hope to be acting from love rather than fear, vanity, power, or superstition. When we begin with the realization that all of life, including each mundane detail of living as a family, is sacred, we're no longer in a battle with our surroundings, trying to impose holiness on them. Rather, we become humble students, apprentices in love, disciples of the ordinary who seek the face of God in our homes.

How do you go about embarking on parenthood as your spiritual path? Two qualities stand out as fundamental: Make it real, and keep it simple. Not easy, necessarily, but simple.

Taking action 9

How to be a genuine,

spiritual parent

Practice acceptance. A lot of modern life is driven by an increasing expectation that you should "have it all." Typically this centers on having possessions, prestige, luxury, travel, freedom, leisure, and romance. Compare that to what a parent of a six-week-old baby might expect from life: feeding, diapering, burping (the child), diapering, cleaning, feeding, diapering—and getting no sleep. If you're lucky, you might get a shower in by dinnertime. If from the time you are young, society's great information and persuasion engines (television, radio, movies, magazines) are gearing you up for the "you can have it all" existence, taking on the responsibility of caring for a helpless, messy, demanding, dependent person can come as a shock to the system. Acceptance is an act of the will. You say, "I will take on the demands and joys of this life with my whole heart, mind, and soul."

Acceptance is not resignation, throwing in the towel. It's not giving in grudgingly, like the store clerk who, rolling her eyes, decides to put the personal phone call on hold and, with great disdain, assist you, the customer. Acceptance is taking life on life's terms. It's deciding that living in reality has more to offer you than your small and infantile wish to get what you want when you want it. Acceptance is acknowledging down deep that you are right where God wants you to be and that you have everything you need to live in peace. The outcome of such acceptance is amazing. As David Thomas wrote in *Family Perspectives Journal,* "In the audacious belief that God's presence remains with us, we can do crazy, loving things like giving our lives for others. And this kind of crazy love happens in the intimate life of families every day."

Keep showing up. Raising kids is not for those who crave immediate gratification. For parenting to be a spiritual path, you have to be in it for the long haul. Sure, there are the golden moments when life is sweet and full and the family is in harmony. These are great and luscious gifts to be savored like sweet cherries in season. But raising kids is no overnight process.

They need our physical presence. They need our powers of observation—they need us to keep an eye on them. They need our moral presence shaping their lives. They need our knowledge to answer the question "How does the world work?" and our wisdom to answer the question "Why are we here?" Our presence during those years is what our kids need the most, and it is what we need for our own spiritual growth and development.

When we show up in life, it allows our kids to show up too. This commitment doesn't mean you have to become one-dimensional, living only for your kids. When you show up, arrive as a fully functioning, well-rounded adult who has friends, is involved in the community, knows how to have fun, and pursues his or her own interests. That's the person you show up as. You don't have to be with your kids every hour of every day. But show up regularly and at important times, like at dinnertime.

Be open. I love the line in the Bible that says, "And Mary treasured all these things in her heart." A lot of surprising events came Mary's way, not the least of which was the discovery that she was "with child" and, oh, what a child! She encountered many joyful, sorrowful, and glorious mysteries in the course of being a parent, and perhaps her greatest example is that she found a way to be open to all those mysteries. Not to understand them or to control the outcomes, but to be open to them.

GREAT EXPECTATIONS

When a new baby is on the way, we say that we're "expecting." It's a great word that conveys more than simply waiting for the day of delivery. We have great expectations for ourselves, for the child, and for our family. *Expectation* connotes an openness to whatever lies ahead as we encounter this new person who arrives at our home as a stranger and develops as a unique person every day from then on.

When I think of expectations, I think of the shepherds and kings who came to the manger. What were they expecting to see? A king, a royal court, someone of power and circumstance? That may have been what they expected, but what did they find? Perhaps the real Christmas miracle is that these shepherds and magi did not go away disappointed in what they found—an impoverished couple in dingy surroundings, with no place to lay their newborn except a manger where donkeys ate. In fact, the baby's visitors came away with faith.

We parents need to be open to the possibility that our own "manger moments" can bear Christ to us. We need to cultivate an openness that makes room for God's love and mercy to work in our lives. We need an openness that does not overlook the sources of strength that are available to us. And we need an openness that is willing to sit and ponder and wrestle with the contrariness of the message that Jesus offers—a message that on the surface appears foolish, unappealing, unrewarding, and difficult.

Being open to our kids—not pigeonholing them or stifling their true selves—can point the way to spiritual growth. When we are open to them, they in turn open up to us in trust, a trust that reveals God.

Taking action 10

How family members

can be open with one another

Ask for help from God and other people. Other people are often the conduits of God's messages and God's immediate help. They offer us the opportunity to love others and to learn about those foibles in us that block us from the free flow of God's love. Other people offer us the opportunity to receive love and mercy and comfort and wisdom. This is particularly true of people you admire who have raised healthy kids. Latch on to them and learn from them, almost by osmosis. Accept help, even when it comes in a form you don't expect or want.

You need to do your own inner work so that you are free, solid, and able to be there for your kids. This may involve getting professional help in addition to presenting yourself regularly to God's grace.

When you ask God for help, be prepared to do your part. I used to pray and then wait for God to manipulate life like pieces on a chessboard. Now I realize that I need

to pray sincerely, muster up the willingness to accept the help however it comes, and then take action. I go about doing the next right thing in front of me. If there are many possible things to do, I listen to the still, small voice within that points me in a direction. I try to let go of the worry and act as if the answer is on its way. It always is, and by creating space in my life for God's help, I recognize it when it comes.

Find the humor. This bonus element is crucial to a family's spiritual life. Whether it's out of insecurity in their ability as parents, worry over their authority, fear for their kids' welfare, or simple overwork, too many parents are grim! Their interactions with their kids, especially once the kids hit the middle-school years, are joyless.

Make room for humor, whether it's allowing your kids to be silly or it's being silly yourself. Realize that a good laugh is a wonderful social lubricant, getting the family through rough times and soothing hurt feelings with good-natured fun. Humor can disperse anxiety and rancor and let the light of happiness into our relationships. Being able to see the funny aspects of family life is healthy, especially when we're able to laugh at ourselves. A good laugh in a tense moment lets us all know that, while life together is important, it needn't be all that serious.

There is no enlightenment outside daily life.

Thich Nhat Hanh

Just be sure that the laughter is not purchased at one family member's expense. Humor should bring us to-gether, not help a few of us gang up on one of us.

*Wisdom is knowing
what to do next, skill is
knowing how to do it,
virtue is doing it.*

DAVID STARR JORDAN

CHAPTER EIGHT

From Patience to Hope

Spiritual Virtues Every Parent Needs

I witnessed a quintessential parenting moment when I was at the zoo one day with my kids. I spied a woman across the way struggling with an infant in a stroller while trying to corral two other toddlers. One toddler stood there whining, the other one was angling toward the panther's cage, and the baby in the stroller slam-dunked her bottle into the dirt. The mother stopped in her tracks, looked to the heavens, and uttered, "Lord, give me strength!" before scurrying to tend to her kids again.

Parents do need strength. The Latin word for strength is *virtus*, from which we get the word *virtue*. Religious scholars define virtue as a habit or established capability for performing good actions. St. Thomas Aquinas divided virtue into two groups: natural (acquired and increased by repeating good acts) and supernatural (given with grace by God). We parents need both kinds.

I'M TIRED OF BEING THE ADULT

I suspect that every parent says to herself or himself from time to time, "I'm tired of being the adult!" I know I have. I remember one Sunday morning when I was a young parent and our basement flooded after a big storm. Reluctantly, I was in the dankness of the basement, cleaning and disinfecting, moving furniture around, dragging rugs out to dry, deciding whether to keep a sopping piece of furniture or toss it. As I worked, I began to think of the other chores that loomed unfinished: our gutters and eaves needed painting; the garden needed weeding; I'd left a put-it-together-yourself dollhouse half finished, and my daughter had just about given up on ever playing with it; the drain in the bathtub was gurgling slower and slower each day; and I still needed to put that insulation in the attic. At about that time, feeling properly sorry for myself, I decided I no longer wanted to be the adult. My kids were upstairs watching cartoons and eating cinnamon toast. That sounded just fine for me too. But after a giving myself a moment to enjoy that reverie, I poured more Lysol into a bucket and continued sloshing the floor, praying for endurance.

It's a parent's job to hold things together for the family. That takes strength. I worked for a number of years as a childcare worker; I took care of children who had become wards of the state. When I read their files, I quickly realized that the most common reason their families had fallen apart was lack of inner strength on the part of the adults. I don't mean to moralize against the unfortunates whose children were in my care, but the truth is that despite the best of intentions, the parents were not strong enough—didn't have the virtue—to create a safe space in which the children could live and grow. Often their strength was diminished through drink or drugs. Most often there had been long-term poverty, and that was typically complicated by another blow to the family, such as an untimely death or the onset of severe depression. When I say there was a lack of strength, I don't mean that there was a lack of power exhibited. There was often a lot of corporal punishment meted out. Often, when there was an absence of real inner strength, a kind of macho display of raw power substituted. But whatever power was there was not put at the service of the family, and the family fell apart as a result.

Watching a family unravel teaches valuable lessons about the very practical need for virtues such as reliability, perseverance, prudence, and constancy.

Most families aren't under as severe a strain as the families I came to know during my days working in child care. But we all face hardships and woe. And virtues are the pillars that hold up our homes.

St. Thomas Aquinas taught that humans have a natural inclination to justice, temperance, and courage, but we need to start *acting* justly, temperately, and courageously if we want those inclinations to become virtues. In other words, when it comes to our good inclinations, we use 'em or lose 'em.

What are the virtues that parents need to practice in raising children with faith? Here are four central Christian virtues and some ideas on how they apply particularly to parents.

GIVE ME PATIENCE IN A HURRY

A guy I know has trouble being patient. In fact, his inability to be patient has made him a patient—three times for bypass surgery. Doctors tell him his bad dietary habits didn't help, but what caused most of his heart problems is his type A personality. He's chronically ticked off. Or at least he used to be.

Things are changing for Bob ever since a significant cab ride. He was on his way to his "rage management" class (I am not kidding about this) when the cabdriver failed to give him change fast enough. He commented, crudely, to the effect that the cabdriver was not very competent at his job. The driver grunted and slowed down further. This prompted Bob to comment about the driver's parentage and country of origin. From there, it got ugly.

"I suppose it was when I was climbing over the front seat of the cab, trying to grab the change out of the guy's hands, knowing I'm going to get into a fistfight with this guy, that I was blessed with an out-of-body experience. I got a glimpse of myself as if from about twenty feet above. I looked down at this imbecile (me) and thought, 'Is this how it's going to end?' Actually, it was the beginning for me of a new way of living. I've still got a long way to go, but I'm not a maniac like that anymore. I've been given the grace of having more patience than I ever hoped to have."

Being a parent can try your patience. If you've ever taken a walk with an eighteen-month-old and hoped to make any kind of progress, you know the meaning of the word *impatient*. Or if you've ever gone out of your way to really please one of your kids with a special day and special treats, only to hear cries for more, you know the meaning of *impatient*. (Once, walking out of a kiddie matinee at the local theater, I witnessed a four-year-old pointing at the candy display and crying while her exasperated young mommy screamed, "I don't care! I just don't care!" The film we'd all just seen: *The Care Bear Movie*. I guess Mommy was Grumpy Bear that day.) If you've worked hard to teach your child manners and then watch him and his friends grabbing handfuls of food from a lovely buffet, you know the meaning of the word *impatient*.

The natural first instinct is to pray that the others around us will change, that the eighteen-month-old will no longer be fascinated by every dandelion or shiny object along the path, that the child will become grateful and say, "No, Mom, you've already given me way too much!" and the teenager will act like a magna cum laude graduate from charm school. But that won't happen. The immediate situation isn't likely to change, but *we* can change.

My wife once wondered aloud, "Why is it that when I pray for patience, what God keeps sending me are opportunities to be patient?" It takes practice to develop patience. And isn't that a catch-22 for impatient people: "Lord, give me patience and give it to me NOW!"

The *New Catholic Encyclopedia* says about patience, "The primary action that flows from this virtue is to endure: thus patience is annexed to the virtue of fortitude." Notice that it doesn't say that patience makes life conform to your desires. The arrival of patience allows you to endure what seemed unendurable. Sometimes that's the best that a parent can do. When you're at the end of your rope, patience helps you hang on.

The *New Catholic Encyclopedia* goes on to say that contrary vices to patience include insensibility. In family life, the real downside of impatience is that it leaves a parent unmoved by the plight of another. So I yell at my kid who is whining, only to find out a few hours later that she was coming down with a bad cold. Or I make a cruel remark about how long it takes my daughter to get ready for a dance, not realizing that she's had a horrible day and her sense of self has taken a beating. Or I can't wait an extra minute to get at a project hanging over my head and thus am oblivious to the clues from my daughter that she could use a shoulder to cry on or someone to give her feedback.

A bout of impatience tells me I'm not living in the moment. On the contrary, I'm way ahead of myself. I want now what can only be gotten at some other time—if at all. I'm divorced from my senses, and I'm living in my head. This helps no one.

Reframe the situation; take the longer view. Most situations that spark our impatience are of no real consequence. Asking

Taking action 11

How to be patient, and soon

yourself,
"Will this really matter ten years from now?" is a great way to put the situation in perspective. Or you can take God's view and say, "In light of eternity, how important is this?"

Depersonalize

the situation. Stop and remember that odds are what's bothering you is not directed at you. If the computer freezes, it hasn't chosen to do this to you specifically. You just happen to be the handy idiot trying to make it run.

Kids tend to personalize their complaints when they're tired, frustrated, or feel powerless. It can really sting to hear "I hate you!" but such comments are rarely about us as parents. We're simply handy targets for our kids' frustration. Better you should let the comment bounce off you and get curious (lose your insensibility) and ask, "I wonder what's going on that she would say that?" Then follow up with a wonderful lesson in not retaliating in kind. This lesson came

in handy when my younger daughter was just weeks old. She suffered from colic, and we spent many a night pacing the rooms of our small house, since occasionally she was comforted when we walked while holding her close. But mostly she cried. It was a cry of pain—and a pain to hear. Kathleen and I were exhausted and anxious. It was easy to take the crying personally, as though there were something we could do but had failed to do. But learning more about colic, about the continuous stomach spasms and cramps, we came to understand the physical cause of these painful symptoms. It became easier to endure the long sessions of pain with compassion rather than impatience.

Concede the argument.

Having to constantly defend your decisions to your kids can be a major source of impatience. Family-life expert Dolores Curran offered great advice for parents whose patience runs out with kids who want to argue every point of family policy. "When my son would say to me, 'That's not fair!' I would simply say, 'You're right. Now go do what I told you.'" Sometimes, arguing won't help anyway, so just skip that step.

Give yourself a break. Mark Twain once said, "I've known a lot of trouble in this life, most of which never happened." Does your self-talk tend to "catastrophize" and lean toward worry? Do you berate yourself mercilessly for any minor, normal, human mistake? Does your inner dialogue sound like that mincing announcer on the figure-skating broadcasts who criticizes every untucked elbow or unpointed toe (and this for the five or six most talented skaters in the world!)? Why not let yourself off the hook? Otherwise, you will begin to treat others as shabbily as you treat yourself, and no one deserves that.

Accentuate the positive. Every fault we have has a flip side that is a blessed strength. Yes, you may be impatient at times, but you may also be strong on persevering, promoting justice, or protecting the underdog. I suspect that when you exercise the positive aspect of this two-sided coin, you will have less trouble with the negative side. As long as you can moderate your impatience, it's a small price to pay for the good that flows from that strength.

Be patient with yourself. The only way to acquire patience is to practice that virtue. Do it consciously but not obsessively. And take your time with it. Exercise gentle curiosity. Take note of what emotions come up when you call on yourself to be patient. These can be clues to what's missing in your life or what's out of step in your life—things that spur your impatience. Bringing these inner motivations to the light of God's gaze can help them heal and diminish in power.

FEAR OF THE LORD TAKES COURAGE

The Old Testament calls fear of the Lord the beginning of wisdom. The word *fear* as used here is not meant to foster the suspicion that God is out to get you or that if you make one false move, you're done for. The term *fear* as used here signifies a wake-up call, a breakthrough event that reveals God as awesome—that is, worthy of awe. Rather than pointing to God as a petty tyrant, true fear of the Lord opens our eyes and our hearts to the reality that God is majestically good—beyond our full comprehension but worthy of our adoration and our longing. Experiencing fear of the Lord changes our focus and raises our sights. After such an experience, we are no longer content to live life on the surface; we want to go deeper and engage life at the level where God meets us and where we are most human. Fear of the Lord lets us know that when we approach God, we encounter a power greater than ourselves, whose ways are not necessarily our ways but whose ways lead to eternal life. It's an invitation to the life we are called to live.

The Bible serves up many images of God that reflect the various human experiences of God. Some are comforting, like the solicitous father who welcomes the prodigal, the mother hen who worries over her chicks, or the gentle shepherd who seeks out the lost sheep. The images of God connected to the experience of fear of the Lord run more to the burning bush, the thundering voice from the cloud, or the One in the Garden who demanded of Adam and Eve, "Who told you that you were naked?"

The Lord who inspires such fear is Michelangelo's *God of Creation* and *Last Judgment*. This is the God who answered Job's plaintive cries by blasting out, "Where were you when I created the seas and the skies, the mountains and the plains?" Before that question, Job was complaining. After that, he sat silent but had a chance to grow in wisdom. Job may not have gotten direct answers to the questions he was asking, but he got a clear sense that there were other questions more worth pondering. Such fear of the Lord gave him something else to think about: "I've been living my life unaware of this larger reality until now."

When I think of fear of the Lord, I recall an incident that happened while I was a camp counselor and child-care worker at Maryville Academy, an orphanage outside Chicago. One of my charges—let's call him Jimmy—was an angel-faced five-year-old who swore like a stevedore and resisted all efforts to civilize him. I was having trouble getting him to see my point of view one day out in the play yard. In fact, he was throwing a tantrum and swearing up a storm. When I asked him to sit down next to me, he shouted something crude and ran from me, escaping around the corner into the girls' play yard. What happened then was like a cartoon, because the next thing I saw was Jimmy, stiff as a board, retracing his steps backward into the boys' yard again. In front of him, matching him step for step, was Father John Smyth, the superintendent of the home.

Smyth had been an all-American on the University of Notre Dame's basketball team and had been drafted by the St. Louis pro team before he joined the seminary. He stands well over six feet tall, has hands like the paws of a giant grizzly and eyes that look right through you. There's no one more dedicated to the welfare of Maryville's kids or more loving. But neither can I think of anyone more able to convince an incorrigible five-year-old that it might be time to rethink his ways. That comic pantomime—the huge, lumbering priest walking toe-to-toe with the tiny imp of a boy—had me almost laughing out loud.

Then Smyth sat Jimmy down, and they had a little heart-to-heart talk. Somehow new ideas got through to Jimmy; he began to see that there were concerns in the world other than his. There were larger, more central, more fundamental questions to deal with than his transitory wishes. They may have talked about issues like listening to the counselors and behaving in the play yard, but the real issue was that Jimmy needed to acknowledge a power greater than himself. Smyth got his attention and his respect. There may have been fear involved, but that fear was simply the beginning of looking at life in a less ego-centered way. Jimmy was embarking on the beginning of wisdom.

Many family events can provoke awareness of this virtue. It often happens at the birth of a new child and thus is akin to awe. It happens at the unexplainable death of a loved one, particularly someone who dies too young. It can happen at times of closeness or when life seems its bleakest. Fear of the Lord can be prompted when we stop to ponder, "What words do I want on my tombstone?" Whenever the illusion that we are self-made and self-sustaining creatures breaks down, fear of the Lord becomes possible. "God is close to the brokenhearted."

Fear of the Lord is a great antidote to the "whatever" syndrome. (Mom to teenager: "You've got to learn to take a stand on what you believe." Teenager: "Whatever.") Fear of the Lord helps us keep our top priorities in focus: "Seek ye first the kingdom of God." It helps us shake loose peripheral questions and experiences in a down-deep way that rouses fundamental existential questions: "Why am I here and what do you want from me?"

Fear of the Lord doesn't mean you can't stand toe-to-toe with God, demanding to encounter God's fullness. When we sense the magnitude of God, our lives grow larger as well. The scene in *Forrest Gump* when a crippled, depressed, demoralized Lieutenant Dan lashes himself to the mast, fist pumping angrily at God, during a horrendous storm at sea brings fear of the Lord to mind. Standing up to this awesome God was the first step in the recovery of Lieutenant Dan's life and joy. It's an expression of the reality that our God is a God to be reckoned with.

This attitude of reckoning fiercely in the face of God's enormity is captured in a story from Myron Cohen, the late, great Jewish vaudeville comic. A grandmother was walking down the beach on a beautiful day with her grandson. Out of nowhere, a huge wave came along and swallowed the little boy up and took him out to sea. The Jewish grandmother put one hand on her hip and with the other waved a finger to the heavens as she informed God, "I want that boy back here immediately!"

Again, seemingly out of nowhere, a giant wave formed and crashed on the beach, and standing there, sopping wet but none the worse for wear, was the little grandson. The old woman looked him over, up and down. She struck her fearsome pose again and, glaring up at the heavens, demanded, "He had a hat!"

The basic dynamic behind fear of the Lord is coming to know our place. It's the recognition that we are wondrous creatures but that God is the creator. In an article in the magazine *Commonweal,* Patrick O'Boyle recalled the late-1940s "Speakers Corner" appearances of Frank Sheed, the Catholic author and publisher who would take to the streets to preach the wonders of Catholicism to whoever would listen. O'Boyle reported, "Sheed could be devastating with hecklers. Once, after he had described the extraordinary order and design to be seen in the universe, a persistent challenger retorted by pointing to all the world's ills, and ended by shouting, 'I could make a better universe than your God!'

"'I won't ask you to make a universe,' Sheed replied. 'But would you make a rabbit—just to establish confidence?'"

Taking action
12

How to instill a healthy fear of the Lord

Allow your kids to face consequences. Knowing there are consequences to taking God and our own spiritual life too lightly can help us be firmer about providing consequences to our kids' actions. Constantly cushioning the fall for our kids does them a grave disservice.

Help your kids examine and rearrange their priorities. There's all sorts of pressure to have our kids be popular, involved, and carefree. I'm not arguing that we should try to avoid these things for our kids, but we need to recognize the relative importance of popularity, involvement, and the freedom to do whatever one wants. Too often these traits are sought at the expense of integrity, character, compassion, and self-awareness.

Show reverence; encourage reverence. You can speak volumes if you have a sense of awe in regard to God. Do your kids see you pray? Do you strike a reverent pose—not faked or put on, but sincere? Do you kneel before the altar, genuflect when you get to church? Do you bless yourself as if you mean it, or do you simply wave your arms as though you're swatting a fly? You can't be aware of God's majesty every minute of the day, but does that awareness *ever* exhibit itself in your life? If so, your kids will pick up on it.

Here's a story from George Dosci, architect and author, which was retold in Robert Bly's *Little Book on the Human Shadow.*

> When I was a boy in Hungary I loved dinner. I loved to go into the dining room and sit in front of the big plates, and have the maid come in and serve the soup. One evening I went downstairs and the dining room was in an uproar. A pogrom had taken place in Russia, and many

Jews were fleeing over the border into our town. My grandfather went down to the railway station and brought home Jews whom he found there.

I didn't know what was going on, but I could see old men with skullcaps in the living room, mothers nursing babies in the corners of the dining room, and I threw a fit. I said, "I want my supper! I want my supper!" One of the maids offered me a piece of bread. I threw it on the floor and screamed, "I want my supper!" My grandfather happened to enter the room at that moment and heard me. He bent down and picked up the piece of bread, kissed it, and gave it to me. And I ate it.

In an inspired gesture loaded with meaning, Dosci's grandfather invited the young boy to rise up from an understandable but selfish place to a sacred space. Bly commented, "The kissing of the bread is very beautiful, I'm not sure why." How would you answer Bly?

Respond to

questions about death and the end of the world with the concept that it matters how we live. At certain ages, kids become highly interested in death and what happens when we die. It's a good time to gently convey the sense that while we needn't worry about every sin, how we live will prove a judgment on us. Modern parents find this tricky, so they often avoid it. Not wanting to scare their kids with threats of hell, parents sometimes don't convey enough that our actions matter and that how we choose to live has consequences far beyond the here and now. We need to find ways to let our kids know that there is a purpose to life and a way of living that will lead to eternal life.

PRUDENCE REQUIRES PASSION

Prudence has image problems. It has the reputation of being the ninety-eight-pound weakling among the virtues. Father James F. Keenan, S.J., said, "In our day, 'Be prudent' means 'don't get caught.'" People often think of prudence as caution prompted by timidity and self-preservation. Maybe you remember that *Saturday Night Live* send-up of the cautious George Bush: "No, it wouldn't be prudent." But, added Keenan, "in the [faith] tradition, prudence means finding the courses of action that lead to moral growth."

Prudence is practical wisdom and judgment. Prudence is doing good through the best choices and means. It's one of the four cardinal virtues. So prudence is actually the applied wisdom that choreographs all the other virtues.

Parents need prudence. They need to have not only a firsthand idea of what virtuous course of action is in order but also a knowledge and understanding of each child in their care. "It is clear that if a parent treated each child the same, then only one child would grow adequately," said Keenan. "Respecting the uniqueness of the person is the foundational concern of prudence. We cannot give prudential advice unless we have a clear idea of who the agent is. In a manner of speaking, a virtue ought to fit a person the way a glove fits a hand. There is a certain tailor-made feel to a virtue that prompts Thomas Aquinas to call virtue 'our second nature.'"

Prudence is being able to say the right word at the right time—not stepping in too soon, but not holding back or withdrawing either. Prudence is not doing *for* the children; it's finding the way to empower or enable them to be virtuous on their own. Prudence is seeking the help we need and making sure we aren't missing something important and necessary to function well.

As the parent, it falls to you to be able to look at the larger picture and do what's necessary to hold things together. Sometimes it's lightening things up with a laugh; sometimes it's making sure a half-spoken concern is brought to light and heard fully. And sometimes it's knowing when to simply let a moment happen.

My young niece Elizabeth told us of one such situation when her dad, Marty, was able to accurately read the moment and was creative enough to do the right thing—which was to do nothing. The story takes place a number of years ago when Elizabeth's mom, Jean, was expecting her fourth child. The pregnancy turned out to be difficult, and Jean's health was at risk. Marty had recently started a new job and was in the midst of grad school. Family members pitched in to care for the kids, but it was an extended time of intensity and disruption of normal family routine.

Then, good news: Meghan Grace was born. We were all thrilled. But all was not well. Jean suffered complications. It was a time of uncertainty and worry. Marty tried to keep life at home as normal as possible for the three older kids. But without Mom at home, it just wasn't the same.

Questions hung in the air. "When is she coming home?" "Can we go see her now?" "When will the baby get to come home?" and the unspoken but scariest question, "Will Mom be OK?"

The days went on, and the tension mounted. Marty took the kids to visit Jean and Meghan Grace. They had a good visit, but there were no certain answers and it was hard to leave the two of them and return to the house, which seemed so empty without them. They ran necessary errands on the way home. Marty was distracted with the many details of keeping the house running, keeping up with his work, and arranging for who'd care for the kids. But on the last leg of their journey, he focused on the kids and tried to be present to them, to their worries and cares.

They talked a bit, made contact, and then a song came on the car radio. It was a song that had been popular all season while their mom was still home and they were all together. Now it conjured up memories of when life had seemed normal. Elizabeth, Bridget, and Brian sat in their regular seats, listening and perhaps singing quietly the words to "Colors of the Wind."

They pulled into the driveway, and Marty moved to turn off the car. But he sensed the moment, and he stopped himself. He looked at the eyes of his kids in the rearview mirror, and he sighed. For a minute, he, too, put down his burdens and joined in the reverie. The words and music filled the van and lifted their hearts. Eyes may have misted, and a tear may have streaked a young cheek or two. But the fabric of the family was strengthened, and the small rip within it began to mend.

A couple of years later, that same song came on the car radio when Meghan, her sisters, and her brother were spending the night at our house. That's when older sister Elizabeth told us the story. She talked about the trip back from the hospital and how they sat in the driveway. "Daddy didn't turn off the music. He let it play. He let us sit there in the van and listen to it all the way through." The light in her eyes and the tone in her voice told the whole story—of a family that felt torn from its moorings and a special moment of grace when hope was revived and courage was shared. That's prudence.

WATCHFULNESS IS AN ART

I know of a golf pro who was very successful, yet he spent most of his time observing. He understood each player so well that rather than remake all his students in the same cookie-cutter style, he was able to make small, individualized suggestions that brought out the best in each player. The focus was not on changing people but on understanding them, their strengths and weaknesses, and giving a word that would do the most good.

Parents ought to take the part of the Hippocratic oath that says, "Do no harm." Sometimes it's best for us to just be silent, especially when our kids get into the preteen and teenage years. At that point, it becomes extremely important for the kids to feel that they have control of the flow of information. It's part of their establishing their own identity. So any mild question comes across like the third degree. They treat you as though you were the Gestapo beating the answers out of them. Hold your tongue. Wait, count to ten, say Hail Marys, or hum the *Jeopardy!* theme song in your head rather than ask the question that you know will put them over the edge.

Ask permission before you offer an opinion. This might drive you wild, but it works. Think of a coworker and how it would go if he came up to you, saw you were having a problem with a piece of office equipment or machinery, and said, "Here, let me tell you what you're doing wrong and what you ought to do to do it right." You wouldn't try that on an office mate, would you? Why not give our kids the same respect we give to those we work with or a stranger we meet on the street.

REAL HOPE REALLY HELPS

Desperation feels like a room closing in on you: four barren walls, no exit. Desperation is a failure of imagination. It's the inability to imagine that God can do for us what we ourselves are not able to do. It's like the man who is hanging from a thin branch on a sheer cliff who needs to figure out in advance how the expert rescuers might save him before he's willing to let them bring him to safety. If he can't imagine it, it must not be possible. Sometimes we won't just let go and let God take over.

Being hopeful is not the same as being Pollyannaish, that is, unaware of the difficulties and tragedies in life. True hope is aware of what horrible things can happen but holds on to the belief that God can redeem even our darkest moments.

Parents need hope. Our children represent the future to us, and without hope we will be left to face the future with fear. If we are limited to our own ability to fashion a future for our children, the future can look bleak. Hope tells us that even though we cannot see around the bend in the future, our children will have everything they truly need.

Children will often come to their parents in momentary despair. The boy who tries and tries but can't grasp his science lesson. The girl who wants so desperately to make the cut of the traveling basketball team but who is awkward and unathletic. The son who has fallen madly for a girl who doesn't know he exists. The candidate for class president who finds out that a former friend is campaigning against her. These sorts of challenges can be extremely traumatic for young people. They don't know enough about life to know that the sun will still rise tomorrow. It's at times like these that parents need to be steeped in hope. Can we contain their worries without getting capsized by them ourselves? Only if we have hope. Can we acknowledge and receive their worries and meet them with a positive outlook? Only if if we have hope. Can we approach life from a stance of optimism so that our own fears and anxieties do not become our children's bread and butter? Only if we have hope.

Of course it's easy to worry about what the world will do to our children. We know their tender spots (even the children who seem so strong and impervious to self-doubt have their vulnerable places), and we know how the world can chew them up. The boy who stutters, the sixth-grade girl who still sucks her thumb in the haven of her own room, the kid with the tough exterior who has such a hard time saying he's sorry, the one who is simply different from the rest. Without a firm base of hope to stand on, we will be consumed with our own anxiety for our children and undercut their strengths and tender shoots of hope. We need a container sufficient to hold all these worries and still remain open to life's goodness. That container is hope.

Hope is not pie in the sky, or unrealistic. Even though we may not be able to envision the opportunities that await us or our children, hope is the well-founded decision to not limit God's power by the constraints of our own imagination.

Hope serves to break us out of routines. Some would define insanity as "doing the same thing over and over yet expecting different results." Often we parents find ourselves trapped in that kind of insanity, repeating certain parenting behaviors despite the fact that what we're doing is not working. Hope gives us room to let go of the pattern that, though familiar, is getting us nowhere. It invites God to act in our lives.

We parents practice hope when we take the longer view of a situation. We practice hope when we remember our children's strengths as well as their current fears or vulnerabilities. We practice hope when we honestly admit we don't know exactly how a situation will work out or how God is present, but we confidently cling to our faith that God is at work in the situation in our behalf.

I have an exercise that helps build hope. Late at night when I'm worried about dozens of things at once, or every new situation I think of makes me cringe because a deadline looms, or I have dozens of difficult phone calls to return, I try this exercise. Here's how it goes: Imagine God, Jesus, or Mary sitting across from you, placidly. It helps me to think of God as being quite enormous. Every time a worry plagues my mind, I imagine myself physically placing that worry in God's lap or Mary's lap. This imaginative exercise helps me find release from paralyzing fear. Rather than being a mere escape, it helps me put things in perspective so that I can take any useful action possible but leave the results to God.

One night when my daughter Judy was feeling harried because she was in the middle of final exams and had a number of research papers due, I suggested she try this practice. And it does take practice. She said she'd give it a go, but we really didn't talk much about it after that. Then this summer, when I had a number of major deadlines looming, family members were ill, and I felt there were more demands on me than I could possibly respond to, Judy gave me a package. "Open it carefully," she warned.

Inside the box was a statue Judy had made. The statue was of Mary, seated, her arms curved around with her hands on her knees. Her lap made a sort of well. Also in the box was a little circular container with small stones in it. "This is like you told me, Dad. The stones are your worries. When one comes along, put it in Mary's lap and let go of it." That statue sits on my desk in front of me as I work. On a typical day, Mary sits there serenely, carrying four or five stones. She is a visible sign of my faith, my belief that I am not alone with my troubles and concerns. She is a symbol of the truth that hope is preferable to fear. And I'm glad that I can learn this lesson from my own child.

Taking action 13

How to get a handle on hope

Be open to hope. Since hope is one of the God-given virtues, you cannot manufacture it on your own. But you can help yourself and your children be available, open, and accepting of the gift when it comes. You can do this by using hopeful language, praying for strength to trust, focusing on God's promises, and being willing to accept surprises rather than "sure things."

Split the work between you and God. This means that you do the footwork and leave the results to God. Often we get paralyzed in a situation because we're worried about the outcome. We may even know what we ought to do about it, but the fear of how things will turn out locks us up. Or I may be quick to act, certain that my actions will have sure results. But then things don't turn out the way I planned. I get angry because God didn't live up to my expectations.

In times like these, it's best to remember this division of labor: You are responsible for your actions; God is responsible for the ultimate outcome. You begin with prayer, asking God for guidance. Then you simply do the next right thing according to your conscience.

This is not an easy discipline. It takes practice to let go of our desire to control the outcome of our actions and plans. It takes openness and trust. But it can be tremendously freeing to stop trying to control that which we cannot control—the outcome—and just take whatever action seems best. In essence, it's getting out of the driver's seat and letting God be God.

Exercise hope as you can. The more you practice hope, the stronger it grows within you. Let your language, attitude, and actions reflect an underlying attitude of hope. And if you don't feel hope, it's OK to act as if you do feel it. In a sense, you're borrowing future hope to get you through the present moment.

Take the longer view. Sometimes we want now what can only happen in time. If we can look beyond the concerns of the immediate moment, we may see a larger story of hope unfolding in our lives. This is the impetus behind the popular books that tell us, "Don't sweat the small stuff (and it's all small stuff)."

Be an unanxious presence for your children. Listen to your children's problems and questions without letting anxiety creep in and take over. Stop a minute before you enter an anxious encounter and say to yourself, "All is well." This is the virtue of hope, spreading out in your life like a fruitful vine. Popular psychology has spread the notion that mental illness can be passed down through families. So, too, can virtue. If we meet our children's anxious moments with hope, they will be more attuned to the virtue that God is planting in their own hearts and souls.

Practice openness to God's action in your life. In quiet meditation, exercise your powers of observance. Look for God's fingerprints

Hope comes softly and often unannounced. It makes no grand displays, but changes everything. Hope is one of God's most tender gifts. . . . Hope knows that there is solid ground to stand on, a hand to hold, a love that's present even when all that is good seems to have vanished. Have confidence. Place your worries, fears, and even despair before the loving eyes of God. Open your heart to hope.

From the newsletter, *St. Jude Journal*

on the events of your life. God may be acting through your own impulses and desires, through the interactions you have with others, through an inspiring item in the newspaper or a situation in a novel or television drama, or especially through your interactions with your children. The more you recognize God's action in your life leading you to deeper love and wisdom, the more your hope will be shored up.

Help your children develop skills of hopeful anticipation while avoiding unrealistic expectations. God's ways are often surprising and subtle. I remember once talking to my sophomore students about prayer. One of my students told me, "I don't bother with that anymore."

"Why not, Gary?" I asked.

"I prayed that God wouldn't let my grandpa die, and he did die. I don't believe in praying." Gary was clearly without hope. It's a difficult situation to respond to. There is no logical way to convince Gary otherwise. The only way to change his perception is for him to become attuned to the ways in which God *does* work in the world on his behalf. Prayer is not a divine vending machine. You don't put your prayers in the slot, push the button, and see your wish delivered down a chute. It's a more subtle relationship than that, and children can be helped to understand the subtleties. But it involves being open, sharing your own experience of how God works, and regularly inviting your children to pay attention to ways God might be working in their lives. Polly Berrien Berends taught her sons, "When we pray we are trying to let God speak to us—to let God give us a good idea." This is the source of our hope. God is constantly trying to communicate the divine self to us. We exercise our hope by doing whatever we can to be attuned to that message, which is life itself.

Read hopeful stories to yourself and to your children. Expose them to the many hopeful passages in the Bible. A good place to start is St. Paul's epistle to the Romans, chapter 8, verse 31 and following.

151

It's a little-known fact that
the real business of parenting
is the upbringing of the parent.

POLLY BERRIEN BERENDS

CHAPTER NINE

From Welcome to Forgiveness

Spiritual Disciplines Every Parent Needs

Children need lots of discipline—self-discipline on the part of their parents, that is. Not only will our children model the good habits of honesty, reliability, and politeness we might exhibit, but they will have a stable emotional environment when we exercise self-discipline. They learn that they can count on us to live up to our responsibility to care for them and to set limits and expectations for them as we do for ourselves.

When it comes to discipline, many parents focus on their children's behavior, but they ought to look at their own behavior first. After all, kids who live in a chaotic household are more likely to be undisciplined, no matter how much their parents lean on them. They'll live out what they see us do. And so it pays to take a gentle and kindly look at our own behavior and, as parents, rate our self-discipline. Here's a quick checklist of behaviors to think about.

- Show up when you say you will.
- Be honorable.

- Don't cheat.
- Don't lie or gossip.
- Exercise your authority fairly and consistently.
- Don't throw tantrums.
- Get to know yourself.
- Do things for other people with no ulterior motive.
- Admit your mistakes; don't make excuses.
- Tend to your spiritual growth.

If you feel you want to make improvements, it's best to go easy on yourself. It's like making a resolution to "get in shape." If you go out the first day and run three miles, the odds are it will be the beginning and the end of your fitness regime. Think of just one area in your family's life that would improve if you had more self-discipline, and concentrate on that for the next three or four months. Seek progress, not perfection.

Exercising your will positively on small things will prepare you for bigger challenges in future years when your child's main job will be to test the limits. The more you bring peace and order to your own life, the more peace and order will (eventually) radiate in your family life.

Here are a few disciplines to reflect on.

WELCOMING: "WE'RE SO GLAD YOU'RE HERE"

The parent's job is to bring the child into the world and the world to the child. The spiritual discipline of welcoming begins even before you hear the news that you're expecting a new child. For many, it begins when you get engaged and talk about how you want to bring new life into the world. It begins on those moonlit walks when you talk about your dreams together, when you practice, in your romancing of one another, the art of putting someone else first. It begins when you create a physical space and an emotional space in your lives for each child sent to you by God. This is fanciful language—"sent to you by God"—but it is true. These children do not belong to us; they are entrusted to our care by the God of love.

Little kids and old dogs know if you're really glad to see them coming.

Anonymous

We need to welcome our children at every stage of their lives, and we need to welcome them as who they are. We need to welcome them with their strengths and their weaknesses, their personality quirks and foibles, their delightful traits and their rough edges. We need to accept the whole package. That means that if you've got your heart set on raising a quarterback and your son prefers stamp collecting, you wave good-bye to your dream football star and welcome the stamp collector. Or if you were always hoping for a little Shirley Temple you could dress up in frills and your daughter tends toward clothes that are baggy and black, you give up your dreams and welcome the reality of the child sent to you by God.

We need to not just tolerate but also welcome our children with their interests and their desires, their shortcomings and their strengths, their ambitions, their temperaments, their sexuality, and their desire to love and be loved.

You need to welcome them when they reach the age and stage that drives you nuts. That can be different for different parents. Some enjoy the terrible twos; some find that stage to be torture. Some people have the hardest time accepting teenagers, while others love those years together. Just know that whatever stage you find difficult says more about you than about your particular child. This is not bad. It's an opportunity for you to accept your child and learn more about yourself.

We need to welcome our children when they reach that stage when they want nothing to do with their parents or when they want to appear fierce, antisocial, and even ugly. And in all these phases we welcome them so that we can, in the words from *Les Misérables*, "raise them to the light."

Now, welcoming does not mean blindly accepting. If my child tends to act selfish, short-tempered, or mean, I do not have to stand mute about these troubling (for me and for the child) behaviors. But I should not try to eradicate these behaviors as if such tendencies don't exist. Our children are on their own spiritual paths. These problems are their work, not their shame. We can help them by sharing our own strategies for overcoming behaviors that lead us away from God rather than closer.

We are also in the business of welcoming other children. These may be the kids down the block, the friends of our children, even the kids who seem so menacing. My wife and I walk just about every evening after dinner. We live near a large urban high school, so we often encounter kids who could easily be cast as "menacing gang members." They dress all in black, have tattoos and countless piercings, and seem to have scowls surgically implanted on their faces. We make a point, especially with young adolescent boys, of smiling broadly and saying hello. Occasionally there'll be no response, but most often the features of the young person will soften, the scowl will disappear, and all of a sudden a fresh-faced kid will smile back and say a surprised, "Hi." And just as quickly, I'm sure, the defenses go back into place.

Our teenagers need to know they're welcome—no matter how antisocial they try to appear. When they say it takes a village to raise a child, they don't mean that everyone ought to be correcting each and every child. I think what they mean is that everyone in the village ought to see this child and acknowledge his or her existence and belonging within the group. The adults ought to form a kind of circle around young people so that they cannot just drift off, unseen and unknown and unmissed. My wife teaches seventh-graders, and she recognizes that it's important for them to test the boundaries. She says, "I figure that part of my job is to be the wall. They need to crash against the boundaries so they know where they belong. If there is no wall, they will run and run, and maybe we'll never see them again." Welcoming our children is not only letting them be where they belong but also holding them where they belong.

One Halloween I saw it this way:

> A maniac comes to my door with a hatchet in his head and blood oozing down his face.
>
> I laugh out loud and give him a high five. I drop an extra Butterfinger into his bag of booty.
>
> Next comes a fairy princess with matching glitter on her cape and eyelids. I bow before her as I drop a few Kit Kat bars into her glow-in-the-dark plastic bucket. She bestows a smile on her humble servant and lightly taps the top of my head with her silver wand. A mixed pack of hoboes and ballerinas rambles up our steps. Football heroes and ghouls, vampires and Pocahontases, even a few cross-dressing cheerleaders show up. They all get what's coming to them.
>
> I greet Mr. Rogers with a bag of M&Ms, Michael Jordan with a fistful of Snickers (I'm a fan).
>
> A hula dancer, three little pigs, Zorro, and a kid who may be a tornado victim (but who pretty much looks this bad all year 'round) arrive toward the end of the evening and hit the jackpot, each getting gobs of candy that would otherwise make my kitchen cabinet an occasion of sin.

What a treat!

God, help me to welcome these kids with good heart and good hope no matter what frightening disguises they don, when they cross my path in sunless, colder days to come.

LETTING GO: "BREAKING UP IS HARD TO DO"

A number of months ago my elder daughter announced plans to go to Ecuador for her junior year of college. I think it's a great idea—for someone else's daughter! Of course we're thrilled with her desire to see other cultures, learn from other people, perfect her Spanish (which is *muy bien* already) in preparation for working, as she hopes to do, with immigrant children as an art therapist. But . . .

Is this the little girl I carried?

Is this the little boy at play?

Tevye in *Fiddler on the Roof*

But of course we're also terrified to let her go that far away. Who's going to tuck her in when she gets a cold? By now I should be getting used to this. I was anxious when she took her first steps and when she first went off to the park on her own. I was anxious when she rode her bike to her friend's house across busy streets for the first time, stayed overnight at a classmate's home for the first time, when she pulled away behind the wheel of our car—alone—and when we dropped her off at college.

Letting go is an everyday occurrence when you have kids. I know it's crazy to keep yelling, "Be careful!" every time my kids leave the house. My words are wasted on them; they no longer hear my warnings. The problem is that we parents know what horrible things can happen and that these horrible things can happen to our children. Meanwhile, our children seem blissfully unaware of what dangers lurk and certain that nothing bad could ever happen to them. I'm glad God planted that certainty in the young. It gives them the gumption to go out and take on the world with faith and enthusiasm. But I'm left with the need to practice the spiritual discipline of letting go.

Wendy Wright, author of the masterful book *Sacred Dwelling: A Spirituality of Family Life,* explored what it really takes for a parent to let go.

> The twin disciplines of family are welcoming and letting go. . . . Letting go involves radical faith. It means entrusting what you most love to the expansive care and protection of God. By this I do not mean that if you pray hard enough God will keep all the awful things that could happen from happening to your child. Nor that every evil, even evil perpetrated on the innocent, is, somehow, "all in God's plan." But that somehow God's presence is available to us even in the mysteries of human suffering and death. . . . This kind of radical trust in an accompanying God is what allows us to let go.

Each day offers new opportunities and challenges for parents to learn to let go of their children. Each letting go represents a loss to us, a small dying that is painful but becomes our gift to our children. And ultimately the goal of our spiritual journey is a total letting go into God's gracious love. We practice this in small ways every day.

Taking action 14

How to let go gracefully

Don't wait too long to let go; don't release too early. Because the act of letting go is a spiritual challenge as well as a parenting task, you'll have to draw on both spiritual strength and wise child-rearing skills to find a prudent middle ground for your children. It takes a certain amount of inner strength to continue to wrestle with these questions during the growing years of each child. It's not as though you can decide at age three what the rules are and expect it to remain that way for the next eighteen years. It's a constant negotiation.

I remember looking at my daughters when they were five and two and saying to them, "Don't ever grow up. Stay this age forever." But they don't. And each age involves new rules, new guidelines, new permissions, and new restrictions. It's exhausting. One temptation is to simply say no all the time, to draw very narrow boundaries within which your children must exist. The other temptation is to abdicate responsibility and just "go with the flow." I've seen that happen, where toddlers are pedaling their tricycles up and down a block unsupervised at all hours of the day or night. Or teenagers are hanging out at the park, and no one at home knows or cares where they are. And while it's not good to raise our children as hothouse tomatoes, it's worse to make them raise themselves.

The middle ground is the harder path, but the correct one. The challenges are to

- Use good judgment
- Stay aware of the developmental stages your children are at
- Accept that often your children will be mad at you for imposing restrictions of any kind
- Accept that you're going to make some mistakes along the way

Invite your children into the decision making. I know it can drive my girls nuts to ask them to think and make choices when they just want a simple answer. But I think they also appreciate my respect and confidence in them. When faced with a new "boundary" decision, whether about where they can go and with whom, who can drive, what time they need to be back home, or even whether they can go at all, I usually like to invite them into the discussion. "What do you think is reasonable?" is a good starting place. Eventually they will be making all their own decisions; why not give them some practice now?

In the ensuing conversation, I can usually get the chance to explain the values that lie beneath my deliberations and ultimate decision. They get to hear my concerns and respond to them. Sometimes my fears are way off base (usually a form of prejudice against kids I really don't know that well yet). But sometimes they're on target. Normally, I find myself much more relaxed and confident about my decision if we've had a full discussion before I hand down a judgment.

Turn to the experts— other parents. It's hard to decide when letting go is prudent. I think it must be particularly difficult for single parents to know how to play this situation without someone else to consult. Of course, if your values are totally different, having two people involved can be worse, but even the discussion/argument helps you focus your thoughts and beliefs before making a decision. So find other parents whom you admire and who can help you bounce ideas around. Observe and talk with parents who have raised children who are older than your children. They're often pleased to share the benefits of their experience. And when you do experience one of these "little deaths" of moving on to a new phase or stage of life, talk with others who share your values so that you can put this situation in the right context—part of your sacred work as a parent.

I'm absolutely convinced that parents ought to talk more among themselves about such questions as when to allow school dances, when to let their daughters use makeup, and what's actually going on at the parties their teenagers are invited to. From the time children are little, it's important to have open lines of communication with the families whose homes your children will be visiting. I read a story about parents of teenagers who created and signed a pact with such agreements as: No kids will be allowed to drink in our homes, we will not leave the kids unchaperoned when more than three are gathered there (or any time there is a mix of genders), and we will monitor the entertainment our guests are exposed to. Too often teenagers will finesse their parents' questions and concerns about plans for the evening by saying, "Don't worry; the other parents are fine with this plan." If you and the other parents are in regular communication, you can gain strength and support from one another. And it goes that much better if you are in contact from when the children are in the early grades. Then you can be more certain that when you're letting go, you're acting wisely and not abdicating your responsibility.

Ask for God's help. I find it helpful to pray to God the Father as a father. I realize that God is beyond gender, but the image of God as a loving father inspires me in my role as a dad. I think of how the birth, life, suffering, and death of his Son were one supreme act of letting go for the good of all. He let Jesus be who he was—both truly God and truly human—and that was good. And through Jesus' redemptive life, the rest of us are shown our true nature as children of God and are freed from slavery to sin. We can meditate on and pray to the God who constantly pours forth life for our benefit. If we want to be like God, we must learn the lesson of letting go. God will help.

FORGIVING: "FORGIVE US AS WE FORGIVE"

What keeps family life going? I'd vote for forgiveness. Misunderstanding happens so easily; to understand one another is hard work. And in our misunderstandings, our selfishness, and the host of other human frailties we are heir to, we hurt those closest to us most often.

Perhaps the most important function of the family is to serve as a school in forgiveness—in bestowing mercy and, even more important, in learning how to seek it, receive it, and accept it. Forgiveness is at the very heart of walking the spiritual path. Forgiveness is essential if we are to cut through the illusions we create about ourselves. We all want to be the hero of our own story. It's very human to want to avoid guilt and assume a sort of perfection. We create a false self. But in constructing this false self we also create a great distance between us and the God who yearns to be close to us. We need to reverse the process; stop polishing the image, and start revealing the true self—warts and all. It is only the true self that can know the full force of God's love, and that love often arrives awash in mercy and forgiveness.

Because the formula goes, "Forgive us our trespasses *as we forgive those who trespass against us*," let's begin not with how to forgive our children or even how to teach our children to ask forgiveness, but with how to examine what hope there is for us when we parents need forgiveness. And I can assure you, all parents need forgiveness.

Have you slipped? Rise up. Have you sinned? Cease. Do not stand among sinners, but leap aside. For when you turn back and weep, then you will be saved.

St. Basil the Great (c. 330–79), bishop of Caesarea

We can learn many lessons about forgiveness from St. Peter. One lesson is that he wasn't so sure that we ought to get carried away with forgiveness lest it get out of hand. "How many times must we forgive someone?" Peter asked Jesus. And to show how generous he felt, he added the suggestion, "Seven times?" He may have thought he was being magnanimous. Jesus disagreed. Jesus told him, in essence, "We don't play that game. You're wondering how long you have to live in the land of mercy before you can go back to your old ways of settling scores. In fact, you want to keep score as you go along. No, we forgive an infinite number of times because that is what God does. God forgives."

Just a short time later, Peter must have been glad for that lesson, because he found himself in need of mercy. Peter had been Jesus' friend and follower. For three years they had traveled and taught together, and Jesus had revealed himself to Peter as to few other people. Yet the night before Jesus died, Peter abandoned and betrayed his friend, denying that he even knew him. Realizing what he'd done, Peter wept with all his heart. In that act of repentance, Peter began the process of forgiveness that led to a new life of courage and faithfulness.

Contrast that with the story of Judas, who also betrayed Jesus but couldn't accept forgiveness. Instead, Judas thought his sin was the end of the story, and so it was.

If you need to be forgiven, remember Peter and Judas. There is nothing so horrible that God cannot forgive. In God's eyes, we are worth more than the worst thing we have ever done. Being forgiven is not the same as excusing our wrongdoing. Forgiveness is pure gift, and the response is not self-justification but gratitude. When we are graced with forgiveness, a question awaits us.

MAKING MISTAKES: "LET'S LEARN TOGETHER"

To set up the question, let me revive an old joke that has come to mean a lot to me. As the story goes, a carpenter went to confession and told the priest he had been stealing wood from construction sites. The priest commended the laborer's sense of contrition and told him, "For your penance, make a novena."

The carpenter, an infrequent churchgoer, replied, "Father, I'm not quite sure what a novena is, but if you've got the blueprints, I've got the lumber."

What I like about this story is that it poses the question "What will we make of our guilt when we do something wrong?" When you find yourself guilty, you have a choice. Will you build a house of shame and live among the ashes? Or will you work to build from that experience of wrong-doing a house in which you may dwell with God?

God is eager to forgive ("I desire mercy, not sacrifice" [Matthew 9:13]). And often, those who love us are willing to forgive us as well. But while forgiveness is a gift, it's a gift that demands something of the recipient if it is to be real. If you need to be forgiven, you can express your willingness to receive this gift by following the threefold path of confession (or admission), repentance, and penance.

True forgiveness is not a single incident that occurs and is over; it's a process. When you need to be forgiven, you have no control over the outcome. All you can control are your own actions, and the first step you must take is to make an honest and full admission of your wrongdoing.

Admit the truth

Admitting failure is a tricky business. When it comes to guilt and self-perception, our emotional defense mechanisms can play tricks on us. For example, some people are quick to feel remorse even when they've done nothing wrong. They may trump up small slights or excusable missteps into serious sins that demand real forgiveness.

Others hide their shame from their own eyes, though they can hardly hide it from their hearts. Even though our inner defenses try to keep us from seeing ourselves in an unflattering light, our bodies and souls will find ways to tell us when we are living against our values. I find it helpful to talk these things over with a person I trust, someone whose spirituality is strong and well grounded. This friend helps me see when I'm taking on more blame than is right or necessary. He also helps me see when I am trying to minimize, rationalize, or gloss over instances of true guilt. It can be hard and painful to look truth in the eye, and even harder to speak it out loud. But as long as I hide my secrets in darkness, I cannot give God all of me, which is what God desires.

Be responsible

After telling yourself, God, and one other person (perhaps a confessor, spiritual director, counselor, or friend) the truth about what you did, you must accept full responsibility for the consequences of those actions. We need to assess the true damage we've done to others. Like a stone thrown in the pond, our actions have consequences that act like ripples spreading out to the shore. We need to accept that once the stone is thrown, there is no way to halt the ripples. Yet, as Reverend Paul Waddell, C.P., professor of ethics at Catholic Theological Union, said, "Ironically, forgiveness brings freedom only when we acknowledge that our actions are not retractable. Real forgiveness is not a quick fix; rather it is a liberating gift that expects something of us."

This is the time to apologize, to make amends wherever possible, and to do what you can to set things right. This is also the time to accept that there are things that will never be undone. Such acceptance is possible only when we are confident of God's forgiveness. As the psalmist wrote, "Cleanse me from my sin. For I know my transgressions, and my sin is ever before me" (Psalm 51:2–3).

How can you be sure that God forgives you? Jesus described the Father's longing to forgive us in the story of the prodigal son. Though his son acted shamefully toward him, the father stood nightly on the hill longing for his son's return. The forgiveness was always available; the process of forgiveness began the very moment the son turned toward home.

Begin anew

Now that we are aware of the consequences of our actions, how can we go on with life? The responsible next step is penance, which means accepting the discipline of beginning a new way of life. "It'll never happen again" is cheap talk unless we do the difficult work of addressing the circumstances that caused our sin in the first place. If nothing changes, then nothing changes. We need to unlearn the "habits of being" that caused us to sin in the first place. Many people resist the idea of penance, thinking of it as punishment. It is not punishment. It is, in Waddell's words, "the reconstruction of one's life not in guilt, but in gratitude." We need to replace our troubling faults with such virtues as truth, faithfulness, compassion, and joy.

Much good can come from our faults and failings as long as we neither hide them nor make too much of them. We are fallible creatures of a loving God who seeks not punishment but reconciliation. The Scriptures are filled with stories of God's yearning to forgive: the lost sheep, the woman at the well, the prodigal son, the woman caught in adultery, and many more.

If you need to be forgiven, take heart. Acknowledge your wrongdoing, accept the consequences of it, and resolve to amend your life. In doing so, you will know what it means to be wrapped in the arms of God.

Teach your children too

It's essential that we teach the lessons of forgiveness to our children as well, both by example and by instruction. When your children err, don't be too quick to punish. Rather, begin the process of teaching them the way to seek forgiveness and make restitution. If they learn how to be truly sorry and take the steps to avoid ever doing that particular wrong again, they are well on their way to living a good life of integrity, serenity, and true peace.

I purposely began this chapter on forgiveness by talking about parents' need for forgiveness. If we can't deal with our own fallibility, we will make it that much more difficult for the kids to deal graciously with theirs. Some parents overreact to their kids' faults and errors. If parents haven't come to peace with their own failings, any failure on the part of one of their children sets off feelings about their own toxic-waste dump of unrepented sin and unprocessed shame. Other parents don't respond enough, wanting to whisk away the grievance as if nothing had happened. And grief must not be dealt with so cavalierly. We need to respect grief—whether over the loss of others or over the loss of our own innocence and integrity.

The role of the parent is to create a safe place in which children can do the difficult work of owning up to sin, learning to become heartily sorry, and doing the repair work necessary to effect reconciliation. It will not help if you rant at the child, "How could you have done this!" or, worse, "How could you have done this to *me!*" as if no child has ever before broken a window, skipped school, shoplifted, or hidden a *Playboy* under his mattress. Neither is it at all helpful if you are too quick to rush in with "Hey, it's no big deal. I'm sure you didn't mean it. And I'm sure Janey forgives you." Parents, let this be your child's own experience of remorse. You can be her quiet and steady companion. Your role is to be a spiritual guide or coach, not a dump truck ready to heap either shame or cheap forgiveness upon the wrongdoer.

You should review the same three phases of the process with your children: tell the truth, accept the consequences, and change your ways.

TELLING THE TRUTH: "LET'S SORT IT OUT"

The first step, telling the truth, is not something that kids will automatically be good at. Younger kids, especially, have a hard time sorting out actual facts from wishes and intentions. The point is not that your kids should always be without fault but that they begin to learn how to handle wisely the aftermath of their inevitable mistakes. In that sense, mistakes and wrongdoing can be ways to get closer to God. And the ultimate goal is that your children will make this process their own and employ it throughout life.

Avoid the twin extremes of nonchalance and over-reaction. Treat your children's misdeeds as serious but not tragic. The first step is to help them confess or own up to what they did. This is a hard skill to learn. Be patient as your child makes progress in self-awareness. Gently lead her to acknowledge the truth. Don't brush it aside, but don't make a federal case out of the issue. Acknowledging the truth keeps kids from becoming irresponsible; knowing that there is a way out of guilt and wrongdoing keeps them from despair. We are all fallible. Jesus stands ready with mercy. *It's more important for kids to learn to honestly process their sin and guilt than to attempt the impossible task of being perfect.*

Ask the child, "Do you understand what you did wrong?" Have your child explain it to you as best he can. This can help clear up a lot of misconceptions. Sometimes he really won't understand what was wrong with his action; he knows only that it made you angry. As time goes on he should come to understand the difference between "Because it made you mad, Mommy" and "Because I took something that didn't belong to me."

Again, don't treat this step as the grand inquisition of the child. Honor his developing conscience and ability to understand cause, effect, and culpability. And most of all, recognize that a mistake, no matter how serious, is not the end of the story.

The late Jesuit Anthony de Mello told a fanciful story that suggests that those of us who sin more frequently are closer to God than those who sin less. He said we're each connected to God with a string. When we sin, we cut that string. In our sorrow, we return to God, who happily reties the string. But each time a bow is tied, the string shortens, drawing us nearer to God. I like that idea. I truly believe that our sins are an opportunity to get closer to God, but only if we know how to give more than lip service to our sorrow.

The second phase in seeking forgiveness is repentance— feeling appropriate remorse for what our actions have wrought. To live a moral life, children need to be able to comprehend the effects (consequences) of their actions. A lot depends on your coaching of them. If you are reactionary, your intensity will inflame the situation and make sorrow for sin seem too horrible to handle.

You can help by calmly asking questions: "How do you think that made Jason feel when you took his toy? What can you do to make things better?" It's best if children can come up with their own suggestions on how to apologize, do something thoughtful, demonstrate outwardly their inner repentance. Let them try without your help, though you may have to counsel them and coach them with suggestions. The purpose of this step is reconciliation—to make the situation whole again.

The final phase is another lifelong lesson: penance. Often the child will be quick to say, "It'll never happen again." And he may sincerely mean it. But here is a crucial spiritual (and human) lesson: Intentions may be fruitless if we don't add to them wise and appropriate action. We must address the reasons the mistake happened in the first place.

We can help our children greatly if we coach them on how to address the habits and practices that lead them astray. For example, if they are prone to covetousness, encourage the practice of gratitude. If they tend to selfishness, foster the practice of generosity. Sometimes just naming their situation—not in a shaming way—and telling them that God wants to help them with that trait or habit can provide powerful results.

Polly Berrien Berends, in her wonderful book *Gently Lead: How to Teach Your Children about God While Finding Out for Yourself,* described a time she helped her son recognize and deal with envy. The interaction took place over a number of days. She didn't chide her son or pester him into changing. With an inner peace and confidence borne of her own previous wrestling with envy, she simply offered him a way out of that horrible feeling. At first, he clung to the pain and his feeling that life was unfair. Over time, he became curious about this "other way" of releasing himself from the bondage of envy. Together they prayed for the ability to let go

171

of the pain and wait patiently for "the good idea God had for him."

The key is for the parent to be a non-anxious presence, like a guide who has traveled this wilderness before and who knows how to find the true path. In order to gently lead our children, we need to have walked that path ourselves, confident in the guidance of God.

Family life breaks down without forgiveness. We need to both offer forgiveness and request it from our family members. Forgiveness takes what's been broken or strained and makes it whole, makes it stronger.

I let my daughter fall from a swing one spring day. She was an adventurous two-year-old who wanted to swing on the "big-kid *fwings*" (as she called them). I let her. At first I watched her closely, but as the drone of pushing her on that swing wore on, my attention drifted. Just once, I pushed a little too low and a little too hard, and she flipped over and fell on the asphalt right smack on her head. I was devastated. How could a father allow such a thing to happen? I imagined all the dutiful parents on the playground looking at me in scorn. My daughter cried, shocked that her daddy could let her down so.

I scooped her up and held her. I rubbed her head and kissed it. I murmured apologies and soothing words. Inside I berated myself and worried over greater—more serious—parental lapses that would be sure to happen in years to come. I felt unworthy.

At that moment my daughter consoled me. Her eyes were still wet, but she smiled. She looked at me, and I asked if she was better. "Fwing better," she said, smiling and trying to boost herself up on the swing.

I had not been the perfect dad. Though the lapse was a brief and minor one, it stood in my mind for all the mistakes I knew I was sure to make down the line. Yet because my daughter had known love and mercy in her young life, she was able to show mercy back to me as well. God worked through her in that instant, and I knew it.

I suspect that in many homes, forgiveness and mercy may be in short supply. It's hard to give what we haven't got. One reason family life can offer so much progress on the spiritual path is that it provides many opportunities to give and receive forgiveness.

Taking action 15

How to cultivate

a forgiving spirit in your home

Read and meditate on the story of the prodigal son. Picture yourself in all the roles: the forgiving father, the wayward son, the son who stayed behind. (Both sons were in need of forgiveness, but only the wayward son realized it.)

Attend reconciliation services as a family. Make it clear that the work of forgiveness, though tough and messy, is part of any Christian home. Seek God's help and the support of the larger community.

Explain what it means to examine the conscience. We begin the Mass by acknowledging our faults and asking for God's mercy. It's easy for us to assemble in church as strangers, disconnected from one another. This rite at the start of Mass is a step toward making us one rather than a splintered group. Explain this part of the Mass to your children. Invite them to do a brief examination of conscience at this point in the liturgy.

Cultivate a spiritual partner or two with whom you can be honest about your ups and downs as a parent. It helps to get the wisdom of people you think have done a good job raising their own children. They can help you keep your own struggles in perspective and offer you the benefit of the lessons they learned the hard way.

A Closer Look

Bored? Tell It to the Invisible Man

Trudging home from work one day recently, I heard a shouted phrase that lifted my spirits and transported me to pleasant days of my youth. "Invisible man on second," yelled one of the neighborhood boys.

For the uninitiated: The invisible runner is a device used in pickup baseball games where there are fewer than four players on a side and, in the course of your team's turn at bat, you have too few players to "cover all your bases."

As I recall, each game demanded a renegotiation of the rules for how many bases an invisible runner could advance on an overthrow, how many invisible men you could use in an inning, and how you should handle the intricate details of force-outs and infield fly rules. No wonder so many of my generation went on to be lawyers.

I paused and watched the kids play awhile. It was fun to hear the banter, the arguing, the running commentary as they played the game. In fact, it seemed as though there were two games going on at once: the baseball game and the game of negotiating the rules so that the baseball game would be fair, nonlopsided, and interesting.

I was reminded of what family-life expert and wise woman Kathleen O'Connell-Chesto said in a recent talk at the L.A. Religious Education Conference. She rued the fact that kids have so little unstructured time to practice negotiating rules among themselves. Too often the games are planned and the rules are enforced by a cadre of parents. The kids just show up and are told how to play.

I knew what she was talking about. Back in my neighborhood growing up, we had the slaughter rule (if we end the inning and one team is ten runs ahead, we start a new game). For games with a shortage of outfielders, we had the "right of second is out" rule, with an adaption for left-handed hitters. To move the game along before dinner, we had the "five fouls and you're out" rule. And from a sense that people should suffer the consequences of their own actions, we had the "you hit it in the Salvatti's yard, you go get it" rule.

I don't want to paint too glowing or nostalgic a picture of this past. Surely many games ended, like the peace talks in the Middle East, with one contingent or the other storming away—especially in late August when we were all getting sick and tired of one another and secretly looked forward to starting school again. But it seems that life's setup in those days was that kids had strict rules handed to them at home and the opportunity to create their own rules on the playground.

But lately, kids' recreation has become highly structured. I hear of Little Leagues that have preseason draft picks! Soccer leagues hand out schedules of which family is responsible for bringing the orange slices. And "lifetime stats" are compiled on twelve-year-olds.

Worse yet, kids are left to their own devices when they return to their empty house, condo, or apartment. Now it really is invisible man at home.

I'm not griping about Little League or parents who work outside the home. But we adults may be misdirecting our efforts on behalf of our kids. They need clear-cut rules and consequences at home as well as a good dose of freedom to experiment with creating their own rules and games outside.

Our kids need unstructured time—as long as they've been prepared to use it well. Too often, parents rush in at the first sign that the kids don't know what to do. But O'Connell-Chesto said, "If your kids say they're bored, pat yourself on the back and say, 'Good job.'" Children need boredom to lead them to their own imagination, to their own inner resources, and to find out who they are without a schedule in front of them.

When your kids tell you they're bored, tell them there's someone waiting for them out in the backyard: the invisible man on second.

Summer Prayer

Because I've caught crayfish in August in the creek by
   the railroad tracks,
and because I've lolled in a hammock after lunch,
   reading Aquaman comic books,
waiting a full hour before returning to the backyard
   pool,
and because I've chased grasshoppers by day and
   fireflies by night,
watched a zillion stars light up a blackened sky,
and tasted the sweetness of a root-beer float on a
   country highway after dark,
and because I've heard scary stories told, and told a few
   as well,
and walked a wooded path with friends I knew were
   pals for keeps,
and built a clubhouse and played red rover,

swung on a rope to splash in a slow brown river,
rolled down dunes and watched a turtle doze in
    dappled sunlight—
my heart may know why Jesus said you must be like a
    kid before you enter the kingdom of heaven.

*Thou shalt not
have strange gods.*

THE FIRST COMMANDMENT

CHAPTER TEN

What You Say and Don't Say

Are You Telling Lies about God?

I was in line at a local rib joint. An older woman, also in line, was trying to control a rambunctious toddler, apparently her granddaughter. Exasperated, she pointed at me and said, "This here's a policeman, and he's going to lock you up in jail if you don't stop misbehaving."

The little girl was stunned, but no more than I. This cute little sweetheart shrank away from me and hid behind her grandmother's coat. I was shocked into silence, unable to conjure up a way to counter such a child-rearing blunder without making matters worse.

I felt horrible being described as a mean authority figure who would punish little children by locking them away. I wondered how God likes it. After all, people often describe God in those terms, with the result that many of God's children shy away for fear they'll be swooped up and punished. These images last long into adulthood, in some cases throughout a person's entire life.

WHERE DO CHILDREN GET THEIR FIRST CLUES?

Whether you know it or not, parents, you're giving your children their first clues about what God is like. Have you given much thought to the God you're describing for your kids? And it's not only in the words you use but also in the expectations you have of how God operates or of what God has in store for us.

I remember when it first hit me that people in my neighborhood might have different ideas about God than I did. For example, one day a friend told me his mother wanted me to pray for his brother, who was in the marines awaiting his orders for duty. "Sure, I'll pray for Stevie," I said. My friend Jimmy added, "My mom says when you're an altar boy, you're closer to God than she is back in the pew. He'll listen to your prayer more than hers." I don't know why, but even at the age of eleven this struck me as pure balderdash. "No he won't," I argued. "God hears us all. It doesn't matter that I'm an altar boy. What matters is what's in your heart."

But neither Jimmy nor his mother could be dissuaded. In their minds, God ran the heavens and the earth like a big, royal court, with the king on the throne and his power emanating out from there to and through the lackeys surrounding him. Kind of like Chicago's city hall at that time. And they were counting on me to put the fix in. I understood the system and promised to "see what I could do." I did pray for Stevie, but I also remember praying that Jimmy and his mother would understand that God hears the cry of the poor.

Another neighbor, a woman who usually seemed on the edge of hysteria, dropped in to visit my mother one day. Mom wasn't home, but the lady stood in the door and talked nonstop for ten or twenty minutes. One of her comments floored me. She pointed to a statue of the young Jesus that stood on our television set.

"Turn him to the door," she said, pointing. "Turn him so he's facing the front door. Then he'll make sure you always have money in the house."

My brother, Pat, and I stood there, jaws hanging and eyes bugging. Again, even at a young age I somehow knew that God was not a magic genie or a two-bit vaudeville actor. "Give me top billing, and I'll see you get taken care of."

My parents hadn't sat us down to teach us formal lessons about God, but they had taught us plenty about who God is and what he's like. Kathleen Norris, poet and author of *Amazing Grace: A Vocabulary of Faith,* offered a clue. She wrote, "I firmly believe that the way we bathe a child or discuss family matters at the dinner table reveals who our God is."

WHICH IMAGES OF GOD ARE YOU GIVING TO YOUR KIDS?

What images of God do you intend to convey to your children? While God is beyond our comprehension, our tradition offers clues about who God is—and isn't. Check out these common misconceptions to see if you're telling lies about God.

- God as cop: "God's gonna get you."

- God as fairy godmother: "God will arrange for my good fortune if I but suffer in silence now."

- God as Monty Hall: "Let's make a deal."

- God as benevolent (sometimes) dictator: "We are peons at the whim of the one in charge. Let's hope he doesn't get angry."

- God as alderman: "I provide services on an 'I scratch your back, you scratch mine' basis."

- God as absentee landlord: "He's never there when things go wrong."

- Or Woody Allen's God as underachiever, whose usual response is: "Oops, did I do that?"

So what *do* we know of God? Jesus told us that God loves us and calls us to divine life. This concept is very theoretical. More in line with where families are at, Jesus told us that God is like a loving parent, delighting in us, acting in our best interests, ready to respond to our deepest needs. Here are some traits that Christians believe belong to God, along with some of the false features that often get attributed as divine.

"God is love." You convey this by being kind and loving to your children.	"God is out to get you." This is conveyed when you constantly find fault with your children.
"God cares for each person with a special care." This message comes across when you stop what you're doing to make time for your children.	"You're not worth God's time or attention." Your children may come to believe this if you're always too busy or preoccupied when they ask questions.
"God created a universe of goodness and abundance." Your children will learn this if you celebrate as a family and keep an optimistic outlook.	"God created a hard world to put us to the test." Your language in general will communicate this if you don't cultivate the belief that God intends good things for his children.
"Who you are is wonderful in God's eyes." Your children receive this message when you look into their eyes and express your delight with them.	"Who you are is dangerous and needs to be controlled." You convey this when you shame your children for having feelings rather than helping the children manage those feelings.
"God is trustworthy." You convey this about God when you make promises to your children and keep them.	"God is unreliable." Your children will learn this about God when they can't rely on you.

Taking action 16

*How to show your children
what God is like*

Stop a minute to think about what traits you especially want to convey to your children, and think about what qualities you might be expressing instead. God is surely more than we can ever portray, and our children will go on (we hope) to have their own rich relationship with God, who is beyond all understanding. But never forget that you're the first and foremost person to give them clues to just who this awesome God is.

Use a variety of images to point to God. The Bible describes God in many ways: a voice coming from the clouds, one who sits on a mighty throne, a still, small voice in the wind, a mother hen gathering her chicks, a jealous husband, a caring shepherd. None of these images totally captures God, who is beyond nationality, beyond male and female, beyond any idea or image we can conjure up. All are clues, and the broader and more varied the repertoire of images for God we stock our children's heads with, the more they'll know about God.

Use religious art. What images do you have on your walls? Do they present an engaging and challenging vision of God and God's works? To find images that appeal to you and convey the wonder and mystery of God, you may need to expand your search. Some religious-goods stores offer a wide selection for many tastes, but others cater to a narrow audience. Also check out fine-arts and gift stores or catalog merchants. Don't be locked into standard images. For example,

Hispanic, Asian, or African American parents may want to include images of God and other religious art that emerge from and reflect their culture. To expand our own and our children's religious perceptions, Kathleen and I have found it worthwhile to seek out religious art of many cultures. We have a carved African Madonna, a tapestry of a village religious festival from Central America, and a Celtic cross from Ireland.

Familiarize

your children with Bible stories. There are excellent renditions of the classic stories that have not been sanitized and "tamed." The stories are rough and wild. That tells us something about God too.

May I see Thee more clearly,
love Thee more dearly,
and follow Thee more nearly.

ST. RICHARD OF CHICHESTER

CHAPTER ELEVEN

Days, Events, and Seasons

Helping Prayer Happen

In the Garden of Eden, in the cool of the evening, God comes striding, looking for Adam and Eve. "Where are you?" God cries out. But Adam and Eve are cowering in the underbrush. "We heard your voice, and we were scared because we were naked," replies Adam.

"How did you know you were naked?" asks God.

Father Thomas Keating, O.C.S.O., said that this story is not just about Adam and Eve. "It is really about *us*. It is a revelation of where we are." At every moment of our lives, God is seeking us out, calling, "*Where* are you? Why are you hiding?"

Keating added, "As soon as we answer honestly, we have begun the spiritual search for God, which is also the search for ourselves."

So what is prayer? Prayer is the practice of coming out of the woods and presenting ourselves to God—despite our nakedness. We present our needs, our joys, our angers, our yearnings, our disappointments, our hopes, our failures—our true selves.

Prayer takes many forms, from the recitation of established prayers to spontaneous sighs calling for God's help. Prayer can be internal, the praying of our hearts, or external, the common worship we engage in at church. Prayer can be tender like the grateful coos uttered while holding a newborn or angry like the shout of an anguished parent crying, "God, how could you!"

Prayer is a habit of the heart. It's an opening of our lives to the glow of God's love. It's a practice that belongs—under its many forms and styles—in your family.

"The Christian family is the first place for education in prayer," offers the *Catechism of the Catholic Church*. As a parent, you can foster the habit of prayer by cultivating your own prayer life, by instructing your children, and by introducing a prayerful attitude into the events and actions of your daily life. You can take advantage of the feasts and seasons around the calendar whether in church or at home. What follows is a collection of ideas about prayer and family life that serves more as a spur to your own religious imagination and action than as any kind of blueprint. Prayer is communication and, as such, will be as unique and individual as every other conversation you've ever had.

GIVE SOMEONE A HAPPY BIRTHDAY

One of the strongest lessons I ever learned about prayer was when my mother conspired to teach Pat and me the Hail Holy Queen as a Father's Day gift for our dad. My brother and I were young (probably about six and seven). Our weekly meager allowance didn't get us very far in the gift department. Mom knew this was a prayer that Dad would really treasure.

Each night when she'd get ready to tuck us in, she would teach us a line or phrase of the prayer. It seemed that we were practicing forever, and our excitement grew as we committed the prayer to memory. We were proud of ourselves the night Dad joined us and Pat and I haltingly worked our way through "Hail holy queen, mother of mercy, our life, our sweetness, and our hope . . ." Dad beamed and hugged us when we were done. Mom was proud of us too.

We learned a lot of lessons from that small exercise. We learned that prayer can be a gift to another person and that it was a valuable activity that our parents prized. We also learned the value of learning a prayer by heart. There are times, when my thoughts are so scattered and my brain is a whirlwind, that I need the comfort of a set prayer that's second nature to me.

I also came to love the beauty of the words and images, from the opening "Mother of mercy, our life, our sweetness, and our hope" all the way through the stirring finale, "O clement, O loving, O sweet virgin Mary." These phrases were beyond my comprehension when first I learned them. But they took up a home in my heart and aided my imagination so that as the years went by I came to know and experience the truth they contain.

If you have younger kids, why not teach them a prayer that they can recite as a gift to a parent or grandparent? (I'm sure any grandparent would be delighted with such a gift.) Classic prayers include the Our Father, the Hail Mary, the Prayer of St. Francis, or, especially, the Memorare.

This latter prayer is a prayer of comfort and confidence that our family automatically calls on in times of danger or crisis. It's a great prayer to know "by heart," meaning that it's so much a part of you that your heart can say it when your mind is frazzled. When I say it, I break it down into phrases like this:

Remember, O Most Gracious Virgin Mary,
that never was it known,
that anyone who fled to thy protection,
implored thy help,
or sought thy intercession,
was left unaided.

Inspired by this confidence, I fly unto thee,
O virgin of virgins, my mother:
to thee do I come,
before thee I stand,
sinful and sorrowful.

O Mother of the Word Incarnate,
despise not my petitions,
but in thy mercy hear and answer me.
Amen.

LET LENT MAKE YOU A BETTER PARENT

If you want to improve your spiritual life next Lent, the best place to start is right where you are. Many people get the sense (and this is often encouraged from the pulpit and the church bulletin) that if they want to improve their spiritual life, they need to stop what they're doing at home and work and get more involved at church. That's not true. In fact, getting more involved at church, while one possible good among many, may also act as a distraction from your real call: being a source of grace for your family. We all know people who are forever involved at church while their kids are running wild.

Taking action **17**

How to get started during Lent

Let go of a bad habit. What would you list as your worst habit as a parent? Nagging? Inattention? Interrupting? Lack of time? Pick one habit and try, a day at a time, to let go of it. Jesus came to free the prisoners. If you feel like a prisoner to a bad-parenting habit, take advantage of Lent to loosen its grip on your life.

Strengthen a good habit. Take a minute to write down three parenting skills that you're really good at: coaching, keeping a sense of humor, staying calm when everyone else is flying off the handle, taking care of the daily details, seeing the big picture. Pick one and think of how you can put this strength to good use on a daily basis. When the flu hits your household, you know how illness can be passed from person to person. But healthy living is contagious too. Exercising your strengths can benefit those you live with.

Ask God to lead you. Every morning, first thing, ask God to help you be a better mom or dad. You have a mission from God to be the kind of parent your child needs. Sometimes when I'm worried about a difficult situation in my family, I think ahead to that situation and picture God already there. With the thought that God is present there, my attitude changes. My fear diminishes; my love grows. I no longer see it as a "god-forsaken situation."

Think of an ocean liner traveling the seas. A small change in its course will, over time, greatly change the destination. Lent is an opportunity to have small changes in your daily life make a big difference in your family over the long run. Practice Lent, right where you are. It's where God is waiting for you.

CREATE SOUND IMPRESSIONS THAT
LAST A LIFETIME

The late Father Lawrence Jenco, O.S.M., understood the power of music. You may remember the name. Jenco spent 564 days chained and blindfolded as a hostage in Lebanon during 1985 and 1986. In an interview in *U.S. Catholic*, Jenco spoke of how his faith sustained him. "Many of the things that are imprinted upon your soul are from your earliest years. For example, the hymns that came to my mind as a hostage were hymns that were taught me as a child. For some reason they were the only hymns I could remember." Jenco clung to those hymns, and they gave him hope.

This is something for parents to keep in mind. Music and song are effective ways to help your children absorb their faith at very deep levels. Hymns have power because they blend words, music, ideas, and emotions in a way that touches the very soul.

We all hope that our children will never have to suffer such terrors as Jenco endured, but surely they will face many "dangers, toils, and snares" in the course of their lives. We all do. What images, songs, and messages will they call on to give them strength and help them make sense of the world? Will they, like Jenco, have a storehouse of hymns from childhood imprinted on their memories, their souls?

Taking action 18

How to introduce your kids to

religious themes and hymns

Sing out at Sunday

worship. If your kids hear you singing, they will pay attention. (My kids usually shush me if my singing gets too robust. Oddly, they don't mind when other parents belt out a rousing recessional.) Make sure that they have a hymnal to use at church and that it's open to the right page. Even when my kids were going through a time of not liking to attend church, they still had favorite hymns, which I'd hear them humming when church was over.

Sit where your kids

can watch the choir. If your kids are small (or if they get easily bored at church services), it may help them pay more attention and enjoy the experience more. Besides, they will catch the spirit of the singing. If your kids are old enough, encourage them to join the choir.

Pick up some

cassettes of contemporary church music and play them in your home and in your car. Visit a religious bookstore and ask the salesclerk to recommend a tape that's right for your kids. Also, there's a growing body of great gospel albums by contemporary singing stars like Aretha Franklin and Kathleen Battle. The words and power of the music move the soul.

Keep your heritage alive

in song. Sing or play your ethnic Christmas hymns, Easter hymns, Marian hymns, and so forth during appropriate feasts and seasons. Keep ethnic birthday and anniversary songs and folk songs a part of your celebrations. They are important pieces of your culture and surely tie in with how your faith has been a part of the history of your people.

In this age of consumerism, I'm glad that my daughters hear phrases like "Shepherd me, O God, beyond my wants, beyond my fears, from death into life." And in an age of individualism, I like how singing joins our voices and demonstrates that we're "one bread, one body." Singing expands our religious imagination and opens us to the power of God in our lives. Think of the power of a church full of people singing, "And I will raise you up on eagle's wings" when a family comes together to mourn the loss of a loved one.

Father Jenco told a story that showed how hymns can bring about conversion. The second year of his captivity, he and his fellow hostages were being held in the same location. Jenco taught them a song that goes, "Allelu, Allelu, everybody sing Allelu."

"In the course of the day," Jenco recalled, "I would hear the young guard sing, 'Allelu, Allelu.'" This continued throughout Lent. One afternoon that young guard came by and placed something on Jenco's lap. "I looked down my blindfold and there was a beautiful bouquet of flowers. My captor whispered, '*Abouna* [Father], Happy Easter.'"

Perhaps the most powerful fruit of Jenco's spirituality, nurtured in song, was his faithful clinging to a spirit of forgiveness toward his captors. That's something worth singing about.

LEAD THEM BY THE RESTFUL WATERS

It's a parent's job to see that his or her children have the tools they need to do well in life. We see that they learn how to read and write or cook and clean. But have we taught our children how to be productively quiet?

No, I'm not talking about the "children should be seen and not heard" theory of child rearing. I'm talking about nurturing in our children the ability to be still so that they might become attuned to truths they can only come to know inwardly—such as who they really are.

> *Be still, and know that I am God!*
>
> Psalm 46:10

"The importance of quiet time is something that our culture fails to respect," wrote author Polly Berrien Berends. "Overemphasis on competition and social interaction leads parents to overschedule their children with play dates and organized activity. . . . Thus we teach our children to fear silence and solitude—or at the very least we distract them from it. In doing so, we also distract them from hearing their own inner voices and the Still Small Voice that's only heard in silence and solitude. The child whose private, quite time is respected and protected benefits in many ways. She has a chance to develop her own individuality and sense of self, to follow her own creative passions, to learn that she is good company (if for herself, then also for others!), to develop her imagination, and to discover deep inner resources for healing and inspiration. Such quiet time is also very good preparation for prayer."

In her book *Amazing Grace: A Vocabulary of Faith*, poet Kathleen Norris described an exercise she devised for children in her art classes to help them learn about the power of silence.

> I'll make a deal with you, I said—first you get to make noise, and then you'll make silence. . . . When I raise my hand, I told them, you make all the noise

you can while sitting at your desk, using your mouth, hands, and feet. . . . When I lower my hand you have to stop. The rules for quiet were similar: "Sit still so that you make no noise at all."

Some of the kids loved it. Others found it eerie. Norris recounted the reaction of one fifth-grader: "It's like we're waiting for something—it's scary!" But the exercise was also instructive to many.

What interests me the most about my experiment is the way in which making silence liberated the imagination of so many children. Very few wrote with any originality about making noise. . . . But silence was another matter: here, their images often had a depth and maturity that was unlike anything else they wrote. One boy came up with an image of strength as being "as slow and silent as a tree."

In a natural, appropriately stimulating environment (that is, one that is neither too highly stimulating, such as an amusement park or room filled with wall-to-wall toys, nor too bland, like a room with no toys or projects and only a TV blaring) a child will naturally find a balance of activities involving noise and quiet. But too often we overstimulate them with too many sights, sounds, and activities, or we understimulate them with too little human interaction, too few interesting games or activities (as simple as a bucket of water and a paintbrush to "paint" the front steps), and too much passive entertainment. Like Scotch whiskey, snails, and opera, silence is an acquired taste. Yet it is essential for the development of the whole person, particularly the spiritual development of your child.

Make room for quiet. Did you have a place when you were a kid where you could go to be alone with your thoughts? Kids need that. It's an important phase in the development of body, mind, and soul. Author Madeleine L'Engle called them "deepening places." These are places—a favorite corner of their room, a tree house, a spot that's good for looking out the window at nothing in particular—where kids can retreat from the surface of life and regain contact with a deeper sense of self, a deeper wisdom.

Sometimes parents feel uneasy when their kids aren't busy. There can be a temptation to fill every waking minute of your child's day with activity or at least noise. That would be as bad for the soul as a steady diet of pizza would be for the body.

If you ask your child, "What are you doing?" and the answer is, "Oh, nothing," remember that your child's inactivity (what writer Brenda Ueland called "moodling") might be just what your child's soul is craving. I'm not talking about a severe case where a child mopes around complaining constantly or never wants to leave his or her room. (For the moper, the best antidote is to hand over a list of chores that need to be done.) But when your child turns inward, be happy. Important inner growth is taking place right before your eyes. Respect your child's time and ability to creatively do nothing. Give your child space and time to tend to his or her tender soul. Rather than intervene, find your own quiet spot and follow your child's lead.

TURN TRIALS INTO OFFERINGS

When your kids come to you with complaints and grievances, do you ever tell them to "offer it up"? I used to hear that refrain a lot when I was growing up. You'd hear it when you were complaining about a difficult situation: a term paper, a cranky teacher, a dreaded chore.

The idea, as I understood it, was that I could offer up my temporary pains and sufferings for the good of someone living (a sister going through a tough exam, a grandmother who was sick) or someone dead.

The exact details of how this "transfer of benefits accrued" actually works may be beyond our understanding, and it's probably best not to examine it too scientifically. But the fundamental point I take from the admonition to "offer it up" is that we humans are all connected, and my actions and intentions can, indeed, support and strengthen others across the kitchen table, across the miles, or across the great abyss of mortality. In fact, recent studies showing how praying for distant patients resulted in improved health lend empirical support to this traditional belief.

As Father Andrew Greeley wrote in *U.S. Catholic*, "Our sufferings do matter; our pain can help others; there is a unity in the human species that makes it possible to suffer for them. The purgatory story told that truth." It's a truth worth sharing with your children and keeping in mind yourself. "Offering it up" lets you appreciate the difficulties of your life in the context of a greater story—one in which sacrifice transforms suffering into love. One in which, despite all our differences, we are all connected. Besides, "offer it up" seems more positive than "because I told you so!"

Report-Card Prayer

Don't let me rant, Lord.
Don't let me rave.
Don't let the words *lazy, scatterbrained,* or
    boneheaded leave my lips.

I know I'm angry, hurt, and stung by
    embarrassment, Lord.
We parents fear that our children's marks unmask
    our own missed assignments and homework

left undone.
We fear the *tsk tsk* of teachers,
the arched eyebrows of principals,
the terror of the "permanent record."

But this report card is not about me;
it's merely one clue to the truth of my child's life
    right now.
Help me to learn about that truth,
to be a good student of my child's life and times,
and to help this student find balance and focus
    and purpose again.

I know there's only one "permanent record" in our
    lives,
and that is minded by you,
who is all-knowing,
all-understanding,
and all-compassionate.
Thank you for grading on a curve.
Amen.

SAY A LITTLE PRAYER FOR ME

I was saying good-bye to a friend I hadn't seen in a while. As we were parting she looked back and said, "Oh, and can you remember to pray for my special intention?"

In other Christian traditions, this might be called an "unspoken request"—something we need prayer for but don't want to discuss. My friend's mention of her special intention brought back memories. I knew this friend from my grammar school days, and her request was not an infrequent one among parishioners at St. Symphorosa and Her Seven Sons Parish when I was growing up. In school, in the A&P, or on the church steps, people might easily ask one another to pray for a special intention.

Surely those were days of more reticence, when a person's private troubles tended to remain undisclosed. This was before Jerry Springer enticed a steady stream of people to come on national TV because "I have a dirty little secret I need to get off my chest."

So when a person was worried about a parent who was depressed or a sister who was going into the hospital for tests or an uncle who'd run off with his secretary (and everyone was praying he'd come back to his senses as well as his family), you'd pray about it. And because we believed in the power of prayer and the solace of solidarity, we implored our friends to join their prayers with ours and remember our special intention. The intention could remain unspoken, people's privacy was respected, and yet our worries could be shared.

Special intentions speak volumes about the Christian sense of solidarity. We believe that we are all one body, the body of Christ. Inviting others to pray with and for us is a way of enacting the blessed truth that if one of us suffers, we all suffer.

The church gives us many ways to formally join our prayers with that of others. Each weekend we lift up special intentions through the Prayer of the Faithful. Many church bulletins include a section that lists people of the parish to pray for. Hundreds of thousands of devotees of the Little Flower, Our Lady of the Snows, St. Jude, and other saints send their heartfelt intentions to be placed before shrines around the country. Some parishes have an open book near the church entrance where worshipers can jot down a few words about the concerns they are bearing as they come to the divine feast.

Inviting others to pray for one's special intentions convenes the church. "Wherever two or more are gathered in my name, I am there in their midst." This became evident to me when my wife and I were meeting regularly with a faith-sharing group years ago. Always the most poignant time each week was when we'd briefly share a spontaneous "prayer of the faithful." Through the grace of God, we were transformed from an awkward collection of acquaintances—each of us nervous, protective, and shy—into a group of believers who let down our guard, opened our hearts, and experienced the flow of God's love in and through each member of the group.

Cynics may scoff at the practice of asking others to pray for an undisclosed special intention. But I wouldn't be so quick to dismiss folk customs, which tend to carry their own wisdom. What might the value of this practice be?

People who avail themselves of such help exercise their belief in the power of prayer. They know that it is good to expose our concerns, our worries, our yearnings, and our hopes to the light of God's love and to ask the support and aid of our fellow believers as we do so. God is eager to give us all good things. But God can work only when we let go. Declaring our special intention is a way of letting go or at least exposing our worry and fear to the merciful gaze of a loving God.

My friend Ed told me that his family had a statue of St. Jude on the windowsill in their kitchen. Whenever anyone in the family had a special intention they wanted the rest of the family to pray for, they would write it (however cryptically) on a small sheet of notepaper and slide it beneath the statue. The rest of the family would keep that special intention in mind all week. I'm sure St. Jude did too. Today Ed's family is far-flung, with grown-up children in remote states and on distant continents. But hearing him talk about his family's prayer practice, I'd bet they are still connected by bonds of love and prayer and very special intentions on behalf of one another.

PAY YOUR RESPECTS TO THE
SORROWFUL MOTHER

My friend Carmen Aguinaco told me about a very moving
ceremony of folk religion she has experienced. It's a gift from
our fellow believers in Mexico that is spreading throughout the
United States. This opportunity for people to express their
condolences to Mary and to join their own sorrows to hers in
compassion has struck a chord in many parishes and communities.

> *Pesame* (accent over the first *e*) is a Spanish word
> meaning, literally, "I am sorry." To give a *pesame* is
> to present condolences for the loss of a loved one.
> On Good Friday, good manners toward Our Lady,
> who had just lost her son, demanded that *el pesame*
> be presented to her. So, after the ritual of the
> Procession of Silence (carrying Jesus' body from the
> cross to the church for a funeral ritual), people
> would present their respects to the Body of Jesus
> and then approach the image of Mary to express
> their condolences.
>
> At San Fernando Cathedral in San Antonio, this
> ritual took on a new meaning when people were in-
> vited to express out loud their own testimony of
> pain and sorrow throughout the year, telling Mary
> how they could sympathize with her because they
> had suffered greatly. In turn, they also expressed
> their gratitude because they felt Mary would un-
> derstand them in their great sorrow and accompany
> them.
>
> The ritual, because of the poignancy of the cases
> presented, is at once impressive and comforting.

MAKE A JERK LIST AND A GRATITUDE LIST

I have a friend who helps me realize when I'm veering off the spiritual path and becoming a maniac. He'll say, "Time to make the jerk list."

This is shorthand for a practice he uses when he finds himself complaining about everything and everybody. He says, "Take out a pen and paper and list the people who are really ticking you off right now. If without thinking hard you can list nine people, cross off those names and write your name at the top of the list." That's your jerk list. It's a good exercise. If there's a problem everywhere you go, think about it. The one constant element in all of those situations is *you.*

Rather than finding this exercise aggravating, I find great relief in it. Sometimes just locating the source of the problem—my attitude—is enough to begin a major change. After I finish my jerk list of one, I rip off that sheet, toss it in the trash, and begin another list. This one is soothing, uplifting, and utterly transforming. It's my gratitude list.

I use my imagination and begin listing things—large and small—I'm grateful for. Everything ranging from the birth of my kids to the great hot dogs they sell at Papa Falco's down the street from my office. I made a promise not to repeat the same things over and over, and I've been delighted to find that there are always new things to be grateful for: a coworker's sense of humor, the way the sun shines in our front windows early each morning as I wake up, the cute old couple who attends the family Mass and participates with joy and smiles for everyone. The list is endless. Only my vision keeps me from seeing the wonders of the world. When I'm too busy looking out for jerks, I miss the beauty all around me.

John Shea said that we don't see what's out there; we see who we are. That's why Jesus could look at lepers and prostitutes and demon-filled people and see the image of God. He saw what *he* was wherever he looked.

By training ourselves to see with eyes of gratitude, that lovely and grace-filled world out there reflects a truth about our own selves. *We* are lovely, and we are filled with grace.

Introduce your children to the practice of gratitude. As you sit around the table for dinner, ask everyone to mention one thing he or she is grateful for. If a child is troubled or out of sorts, see if she's ready and able to make a gratitude list of her own. Make a game of it, with each person taking a turn and no one allowed to repeat something that's already been said. This is a good game to play in the car on the way to a meeting or situation that your child is afraid to face. Gratitude drives out fear and opens our lives to sources of power we might otherwise overlook.

And on Thanksgiving, let people around the table tell a story of what they're most grateful for in the previous year. We've done this at our home, and it's a way of making vivid the reason for the day, educating our children to the ways of family, friends, and relatives, and bringing us all closer together.

A Closer Look

Forty Ways to Foster Prayer in Your Home

What did St. Paul mean when he said we should "pray unceasingly"? Should we all join a monastery? Or maybe he was talking to people who are perennially in need of prayer, like Chicago Cubs fans. If we look carefully, our daily lives offer infinite opportunities to pray nonstop. Here are forty that came to my mind. Add your own to the list.

1. Teach your children one of the classic prayers.

2. Pray before meals together, whether a standard prayer or a spontaneous one.

3. Substitute a short prayer for any "expletive deleted's" you might use. Better your children hear "God bless it" than a close alternative.

4. Pray spontaneously with your children at bedtime.

5. Say an Our Father whenever you start a long car trip.

6. Create a May altar in your home with a statue of Mary surrounded by flowers.

7. Buy or make a beautifully scripted prayer or Bible verse and hang it on a wall in your home.

8. Commemorate the anniversary of a loved one's death by praying for him or her.

9. Keep a prayer jar for special prayer intentions or requests.

10. Start your day with a time of quiet prayer or meditation; encourage your children to do so also.

11. Visit the cemetery and pray for your dearly departed.

12. Have everyone in the family take turns praying for one of the other family members during the day for a whole week. Switch prayer partners every week.

13. Pray for the president, your congressional representatives, your mayor, and other civic officials.

14. Pray for church leaders and your parish clergy and ministers.

15. Imitate the great saint Dorothy Day, who spent time praying for those who were so forlorn that they were about to commit suicide at that moment.

16. Find out when a family member's important meeting or test is and remember to pray at that time.

17. Turn every worry that drifts into your thoughts into a prayer.

18. Pray for every person who is a source of resentment for you.

19. Pray for the person who cuts you off in traffic.

20. Pray for the person who is the subject of a juicy rumor (instead of passing the gossip on).

21. Pray for people who are homeless or down on their luck. (Slipping them a buck or two also constitutes praying.)

22. Sing your favorite hymn from church while driving in the car, showering, or doing housework.

23. Pray while you're reading the newspaper.

24. Pray for the person in need when you hear an ambulance's siren.

25. Pray for a teacher you are grateful you had when you were in school.

26. Pray for a teacher you are grateful your child has now.

27. Give thanks at mealtimes for the farmer who grew the food, the workers (often grossly underpaid) who picked the crops, and the people who processed, handled, delivered, and sold the food. Thank God for the sun and soil and water that made it possible.

28. Pray at bedtime for someone who did a kindness to you today.

29. Visit family members in a nursing home and pray with them.

30. Send a letter to a distant relative, saying you remember him or her in your prayers.

31. Say a simple, short prayer like "Thank you, God, for all the fun that Robbie had today and for all his new friends" when you pick up your child from a place where he had a wonderful time.

32. Say a short prayer of hope such as "God help me to use the gift of this day to its fullest" when you wake your child to a brand-new day.

33. Offer a prayer when you're facing an unpleasant task.

34. Say a prayer of acceptance when your child exhibits a trait that gets under your skin.

35. Pray for your child when she is facing a difficult challenge (a test, a party where she doesn't know anyone, a first visit to a new park or playground).

36. Bless your child's forehead as he leaves the house. Bless his forehead when he returns home.

37. Say a prayer for the caller who drones on and on. Pray for patience too.

38. Say a prayer that God will be with you and that you will be with God when you feel the need to stand up for what you believe in.

39. Say a prayer when you feel tempted to do something you know is not right or in the best interest of your soul.

40. Say a prayer for guidance when you are at your wit's end and don't know what to do next.

A Closer Look

Peekaboo! I See You!

A few years back, my daughter Patti was playing a chase-and-capture game with a bunch of kids on the block. The game had to do with spying on the other team and involved lots of secrets and double agents and running back and forth. Patti and her eighth-grade friend Therese were captains of one team. Matthew, Therese's much younger brother, was angling to find out the plans of Patti's team. He kept imploring them, "I won't tell; I won't tell." To which Therese, in her own sisterly way, responded, "Matthew, you're not exactly *known* for your discretion."

Matthew didn't know what *discretion* meant, but that didn't stop him from pleading, "I'm known! I'm known!"

I think I will forever remember Matthew as the little kid who wanted so much to be known. We all want to be known and loved for who we are. Yet we're all afraid that if we're known and our inevitable foibles and failures come to light, we will be judged and found wanting.

There's a strain of parenting that fears so very much that a child will become needy that it tries to deny the child's needs—and tries to get the child to deny them too. For example, if I don't want my son to grow up to be "soft," I withhold all softness from him. If I don't want my daughter to grow up to be fearful, I deny that she has any fear, and I demand that she go along with the ruse. To avoid having a child grow up craving pleasure, I mete out pleasure like Scrooge doling out money (at least before his glorious conversion experience).

Ultimately this is a fear of being, and letting others be, the individuals God created. It's a fear of who we really are. Sometimes we fear that our desires and our needs will be so strong that they'll ruin us. Rather than acknowledging the desires and needs—and helping our children learn to deal well with these needs—we feel so frightened of them that our strategy is to try to eradicate objectionable emotions and desires. "You're not scared, so stop acting like a baby!"

But we don't really eliminate these feelings; we ask our children to bury them alive. Rather than preventing neediness later in life, this denial leaves the child with chronic unmet needs. Early on, the need might be satisfied easily. But if unmet, the need seems to magnify, and no amount of effort to satisfy it will ever seem enough. The results of this approach can be disastrous. News reports are filled with the fallout of such emotional disconnection.

"When adults teach boys to separate themselves from their feelings," said Geoffrey Canada, author of *Reaching Up for Manhood: Transforming the Lives of Boys in America*, "boys also get separated from the consequences of their actions. Their empathy often extends to their closest friends, their closest relatives, and not at all to people outside of that range. So a boy will shoot up a corner where he doesn't know anyone and feel absolutely nothing." Canada, who runs the Rheedlen Center for Children and Families, a haven for at-risk boys and girls in New York, said, "Starting very early, we need to acknowledge that little boys have feelings, that they

218

are tender, that they are emotionally as fragile as little girls. Like girls, boys need a lot of support."

A child's renounced needs do not go away but are often rechanneled into other pursuits, such as aggressive behavior, which everyone has become alarmed over, or acquisitiveness, which American parents don't seem so eager to curtail in their children. Ignoring a child's true feelings creates a hunger that is impossible to fill. It can start off a round of acquisitiveness wherein the child will want and want and want. The child may even accumulate mounds of toys and games and fashionable clothes but still remain aching and empty. Acquisitiveness, a good and natural impulse, thus gets perverted and magnified when it becomes a channel to bear other unmet needs. Rather than being seen and known and held, the child attempts to feel better through the accumulation of "stuff." This, of course, won't work. The habit of immediate gratification of surface desires in place of deeper needs can lead to addictive behaviors and attempts to fill that inner emptiness with alcohol or drugs.

Granted, it's a tough balancing act to acknowledge a child's needs without feeling obliged to satisfy them all— something that no parent can ever do. The key is not to satisfy all needs but to help the child acknowledge, accept, and handle his or her needs and desires.

Our task as parents in this regard is to be attuned to our children as they grow and change and develop. Remember the game you played when they were infants? You'd hide your face from them, then remove your hands, smile brightly, and coo, "Peekaboo! I see you!" That game goes on, in much more sophisticated form, all through their development. Like little Matthew, we all yearn to be known. Doing what it takes to be in tune with our children is one of the greatest gifts we can give them, and it's also a gift we give ourselves. For if we really know them, we'll see the image of God in them as well.

Prayer for a Left-Out Kid

God, how can those kids be so cruel?
I thought they were his friends.
But they walked right by him as if he doesn't exist.
Every time they laugh about the fun they've had
or boast about the plans they're making,
it breaks his heart, and mine breaks as well.

I want to lash out. I want to shake them.
I even want to make them hurt like he is hurting
    inside.
But more than that, I want them to connect again,
to include him in,
to widen their circle of laughter
so he once more knows its warmth.

God, your Son, Jesus, knew what it was like
to be abandoned and derided.
Help me to have faith
in my child's strength,
in the goodness buried within those other
    children,
in your loving presence beneath all the pain and
    anguish,
in my own ability to be there for him today.

Help me not to abandon him too
by flying off in rage or fear or retribution.
And help me gently point him to the tenderness of
    your care.
Amen.

*The shortest distance
between a human being
and Truth is a story.*

ANTHONY DE MELLO, S.J.

CHAPTER TWELVE

One Story at a Time
A Natural Way to Raise Your Children

Mom, Dad, tell us again what life was like in the olden days." I cringe now to realize how insensitive our tone must have seemed—as though we were asking them to tell us what it was like living among the dinosaurs. But we loved those stories of what life was like growing up during the depression, when Grandpa McGrath was a streetcar conductor and Grandpa Casey was a Chicago cop. We loved learning how Great-Aunt Nell rose through the ranks to become the supervisor of a button factory and what a treat it was when Auntie Bridget would come over and teach the kids to play poker.

Such stories are more than mere entertainment. They can play a big part in developing your child's sense of self. They show us that we're connected to others who came before us and, by implication, to generations who will come after us. They give us a sense of the nature of the world we live in—if it's friendly or harsh—and the best ways for making our way in it. Family stories give us clues to how to succeed, what to value, and how our group defines being a good person. They also give us clues about who God is, especially in relation to the life we're called to live now.

Our kids benefit when they can grasp that we were young once. It can help them to know we suffered the same insecurities and indignities that all children face. Though we may seem all-powerful to them now (at least to our preschool children), our kids can benefit from learning that we, too, had to negotiate the difficulties of school, chores, bullies who lurked down at the far corner of the block, and unrequited love. Our experiences can provide lessons not only for us but for our children as well. When our own kids have suffered difficulties, whether academic, relational, emotional, or spiritual, Kathleen and I have been more helpful when we've shared similar experiences from our past than when we've pontificated. Stories can deliver lessons that lectures never can.

The fact is, we all live by stories. They are the myths that help us make sense of our world and our place in it. Wherever two or more are gathered, odds are someone's telling a story. "Didja hear that they're closing the A&P in town and putting up a tanning spa?" or "I hear old Mrs. McGillicuddy died and left all her money to her cats. Well, don't that beat all!" Unlike *Dragnet's* Sergeant Joe Friday, we don't want to hear "just the facts." We want the juicy details that reveal the meaning to be found in the event. We don't simply say, "The mayor had dinner with the town treasurer." We want to hear, "I wonder if the mayor's wife knows that her spendthrift husband was out gallivanting on our dime with that new treasurer he appointed—the one who looks kinda like Julia Roberts, only chubby."

We tell our children stories of hope and joy (about the day each child was born), of adventures and lessons learned (about the summer spent building houses in Appalachia). And we even tell scary or disturbing stories to help us deal with our fear (about fathers lost in war or brothers who died too young). Stories can lift our sights and our expectations ("We all pulled together and good things came of it!") or speak of warning and danger ("You can't trust strangers and you'd better keep an eye on your friends!"). But, said author Lawrence Weschler, "the thing that's scarier than the scariest story is that there's no story. Generally we live in a chaotic world and the only thing that gets you through the day is the tendency to impose order on it—to turn it into a story. Then you can light a fire and tell stories to each other."

HOW WE GOT HERE

Families tell stories when they get together. I just heard a new story from my cousin Bob at his son's wedding. My grandfather went to England before coming to the States. He got a job tending bar at the White Stag, a pub in London. Grandpa's uncle was in London as well and encouraged him to join him the next day and sign up for a regiment to go off and fight one of England's colonial wars. Grandpa conveniently overslept, which cousin Bob and I agreed is a good thing for us, since the uncle who did sign up was never heard from again. The moral of the story? We may come from the noncombative strain of the family, but we were around to serve as altar boys at Grandma and Grandpa's fiftieth wedding anniversary Mass.

Another oft-told story in our house is how my wife and I met. Kathleen's maiden name is McGrath. We grew up on direct opposite sides of Chicago, she at 5700 North Meade Avenue, I at 5700 South Meade Avenue. I even remember our getting mail to a Jim McGrath—her father—years ago.

I was at a dance at college, and one of my dorm mates told me, "Your sister's here." That was odd because at that time my sister was about four years old. He pointed to a bright, perky, attractive young woman out on the dance floor. "Isn't that your sister?"

"No," I replied. "But I sure would like to meet her." He told me that her name was Kathleen McGrath and that she was in his physics class. "She's a relentless punster. I thought she was your sister."

I introduced myself—she actually asked to see some identification that proved I was indeed a McGrath—and found out she'd come to the dance alone because she had decided to swear off men for a while. Fortunately, her boy boycott didn't last too long, and as time went on, we each solved the problem of whose name we would take at our wedding: We took each other's.

Many of the stories in my family revolve around misadventures in travel, like the story of the infamous Forkin Road. We rented a cottage on a remote lake in Michigan, and the owner gave us some vague directions over the phone. Dad passed along a scrawled version of those same sparse directions to some friends who were going to join us there a few days later. The oral directions said to "go right at fork in road." Our friends traipsed for hours through three counties of rural Michigan looking for the road named Forkin. Arguments still ensue as to who got the directions wrong.

As a parent, you have two important tasks about stories: First, help your child develop a healthy self-story, and second, help tie your child's story into a larger story. Wholeness and holiness require both. Let's first look at the importance of developing a healthy self-story.

AND NOW A WORD FROM OUR SPONSOR

Christianity believes in the dignity and worth of every individual. We are not mere drops in the ocean; we are important in who we are. We are important enough that Jesus suffered and died for us. If you don't have a strong sense of self, you will spend your days trying to find out who you really are. It can be a constant, fruitless search. Without a strong sense of the gifts you have, you'll be unable to contribute your unique talents to the world. I see a lot of teens and young adults casting about, wondering who they are and where they belong. They may vacillate between wild dreams and dreams dashed. They have failed to receive some very valuable information: a sense of themselves and their place in the world.

We parents need to counter the stories that are told by the media. Kathleen O'Connell-Chesto said, "We tell our kids stories so they'll grow in wisdom and courage and will know who they are. Television tells them stories to sell them." Advertising tells them they are nothing without this latest product or that current fashion. Make sure they know that their worth comes from who they are and not what they wear, buy, drink, or eat.

A healthy self-story begins with mirroring. Psychologists have discovered how infants develop their first self-concept: They see themselves mirrored in their parents' eyes. Watch parents with a newborn. See their eyes go wide and their mouths break into huge smiles as they examine every feature of this beloved child's eyes, nose, chin, ears, hair, eyebrows, and eyelashes. Kids who fail to get that interaction with caregivers, without eye contact and mirroring, will not thrive. In extreme cases they may not even survive. Our first and most important messages should be "You are somebody. You are worthwhile. I delight in you. It is so good that you are here."

And the effects of this mirroring continue throughout our days. Think of how a look from your mom or dad can still wither you. Or how a parental smile of approval can make you feel expansive.

Many parents are wary of giving their children too much positive feedback. They say, "I don't want him to get a swelled head" or "She'll come to think the whole world revolves around her." I believe that most children suffer far more from a lack of positive mirroring than from an oversupply of it. We need to give all things their due. What sets our children up for difficulty is when the feedback is nonspecific, overstated, or used to distract from other conversations that ought to be going on—for example, the parent who tries to sweet-talk the child when it's really time to confront or set limits. Sometimes positive feedback is manipulative, an attempt to get the child to behave, stifle her anger, or be nice to others. That's not positive feedback; it's attempted blackmail. Abusing positive mirroring can be damaging to the child, just as withholding all positive response to the child surely is.

But honest, positive, specific reflection from a parent who is accurately attuned to the child calls that child to be his or her own true self, rather than constantly maneuvering for attention and clamoring for clues to his or her worth.

To be effective, such mirroring should be

- Natural, not forced (If you need to push yourself, though, it's better said than unsaid.)

- Specific about observed qualities and behavior ("I just watched how you helped your brother learn that new computer game. You are a very good teacher.")

- Real rather than manipulative (not: "Oh, you're such a kind child. Now get me my glasses. I think I left them in the kitchen.")

- Pure gift, with no strings attached

I suspect that the most common reason parents fail to provide easygoing, natural, positive mirroring is that we are unsure of our own goodness and worth. We would find it hard to hear and believe the words Jesus took to heart as he rose out of the Jordan at his baptism: "This is my beloved child in whom I am well pleased."

For those who worry that their kids will get a swelled head, I've never considered it a problem that one of my daughters might come to realize how wonderful she is, as long as she also knows and appreciates how wonderful other people are.

THE STORY OF MY LIFE

Listen to the stories we tell ourselves. "That's the story of my life!" a man might say disgustedly when the bolt he is tightening snaps off in the engine block. In his self-story, he's a screwup who should expect not mastery over challenges but failure after failure. Perhaps one person's story will say, "I'm in this all by myself, and I can rely on no one else," while another's story says, "If we all band together, we'll be OK." I know people whose story perennially warns them, "Don't get your hopes up," while others live out the story, "God has good things in store for me."

Your child is already developing his or her self-story. It contains much of what you've said about him or her, as well as what he or she has heard from others along the way. It is built out of your child's native personality blended with the accumulation of experiences, attitudes, and meanings gleaned from life thus far. Listen in on little children (who are less guarded with their stories) as they play. Their comments will reveal their beliefs about themselves and life as they interact with one another. "I'm the daddy," says one child who is playing house. "The daddy is always tired," he says as he plops down on a couch. "I'll be the mommy," replies his playmate. "I'll put on makeup and try to look beautiful like the ladies on TV. Then you'll like me."

It's very enlightening to listen in on the stories our kids tell themselves. Are they optimistic? Do they feel trapped? Are they generous or stingy? hopeful or resigned? Do they seem to be the captains of the ship or the ones chained to an oar belowdecks while someone else pounds out a drumbeat for them to row by? In their stories, is God someone who cares for them, someone who's aloof, or someone who sends trials and punishments?

Taking action 19

How to help your kids develop

a strong self-story

Make sure your kids know the story of their birth or of the day they arrived in your family. Why not make a ritual of telling them this story on their birthday each year. What was unusual about the day? Who was there? How did people react when you called to give them the news? Mary O'Connell, writing in *U.S. Catholic,* said that just as the story of Jesus' birth in the manger—accompanied by angels, shepherds, and kings—tells us a lot about who he was, telling our kids the stories of their birth tells them a lot about themselves. "Most children don't come into the world celebrated by angelic hosts and astronomical wonders. But the beginning of each ordinary life is still a once-for-all-time extraordinary event. Telling the stories is a way to tell children just how special they are in our lives and in God's creation—and to give them important clues about themselves."

She told the familiar story of the day she was born. "My grandparents took my father to the racetrack. My dad was never much of a gambler, but that day he won big on the first race. Resisting the temptation to play out the streak, he collected his winnings and went directly to the hospital, gave the money to the cashier, and said, 'This is to pay for my baby daughter.' OK, so I was born before most people had health insurance, and in a time when a hospital birth cost a few hundred dollars. But the story also tells me something that makes me smile: that to my father at least, I was a lucky child."

Tell your kids how they got the name you gave them. What's the significance? Who else in the family bears that name? Was there some person in history whom you admired and whose name you bestowed on your son or daughter?

Relate how your ancestors came to this country (or what people or tribe they belonged to when the new wave of residents arrived). Many times, first-generation immigrants will not want to look back. But kids need to know their roots. My grandfather was mystified with his grandkids' interest in the "old country." When we'd ask him when he was going back to Ireland, he'd reply, "When they build the bridge." From the few clues he let slip, we knew that the journey over the Atlantic was anything but a pleasure cruise.

Describe where your kids were baptized. Do they know who their godparents are and why you chose these particular people to stand beside them at the altar on their baptism day? (It's good if you can give more than a political or economic answer to this question.)

Recount the story of how you met their mother/father. Why did you want to have kids, and what was it like waiting for them to come? (Kids always seem to enjoy stories of frantically rushing to the hospital for their birth.)

Include, rather than avoid, the negative in your family history. Every family has its share of horse thieves and scoundrels. Some just don't have the strength and confidence to admit it. By eliminating any kind of negative aspect from the family story, you end up placing all the "good" over here and all the "bad" over there. When it comes to our ancestors, we need to get the saints out of heaven and the sinners out of hell. Each one of us is a mixed bag, striving to find our way through life the best we can. We can learn as much from the ne'er-do-wells who struggled as we can from the ones who seemed to find virtue easy.

Some people feel that it's best to hold back painful facts about the past, figuring that it will only infect today with yesterday's problems. People worry that information about mental illness, alcoholism, bankruptcies, divorce, illegal activity, or prison sentences might unduly affect kids and should be kept from them. I think this is ill advised for a number of reasons. It would be like withholding important medical information that could help your kids avoid or prepare for a medical risk in the future.

A lot depends on how you talk about it. Surely you could reveal a possible medical risk in a way that generates anxiety and fear. This would not be doing your kids a favor. But you could give this information in a proper context so that they would be prepared to respond wisely and well to any inherent threat. It's in that spirit that you should tell kids about skeletons in the family closet. When information is accompanied by support and shared courage, it can arm our kids to live better lives and to avoid being blindsided by problems, whether physical or emotional, in days to come.

And don't think you aren't already conveying these hidden secrets in some way. Truths have a way of living on in family systems, through shame, avoidance, overreaction, fear, and so on. If we have come to peace with the situation, we can talk about it and be strengthened. It can no longer hurt us. If we haven't come to peace with it, no amount of repressing or hiding will make it disappear. As John Powell, S.J., has often said, "You don't bury your unwanted feelings dead; you bury them alive."

*I'll believe computers can
think when you ask one
a question and it replies,
"That reminds me of a story."*

GREGORY BATESON

CHAPTER THIRTEEN

The Greater Story

Tying Your Children In to the Eternal Scheme

Back when I was a camp counselor, the kids expected me to tell a story every night. After a long day of hiking and playing games and swimming and boating, this was a real stretch for me. It had to be an adventure story with danger and intrigue, warriors and wizards, nothing mushy (these guys were ages five to ten), and a real cool hero. I learned to rely on every hackneyed plot device I could remember from old *Flash Gordon* and *Tarzan* television episodes and from adventure books I read in grammar school. One plot trick the kids always delighted in was the hero who didn't realize that he was really a prince. It moved them to hear that he was stolen from his parents at birth but that those parents always held out the hope that he would return one day. The boy himself suspected that there was something special about him, but he had no clue of his true identity as heir to the throne.

Lots of great movies have that same theme, heroes or heroines unaware of who they are until their adventures lead them to discover the truth—often just in time to save the day. I think this theme is popular because it reveals a truth about us that we suspect but haven't fully discovered: We're children of God.

Once we know *who* we are, we can build on that knowledge to learn life's most important lesson—*whose* we are. That's why it's important to tie your child's story in to a larger, even magnificent, story. Telling larger stories can counter the mistaken and ultimately pain-causing notion that life is "all about me." I think one of the reasons behind the recent spate of tragic events in which students rail against their classmates and teachers and parents is the rage they feel for being handed such a lousy deal in life. They are left to their own devices as arbiters of good and bad, worthy and unworthy, right and wrong. No one knows them, cares about them, or tells them that their talents are needed and important. And no one tells them that they play a necessary part in a glorious future.

It's dangerous to make a child the hero of a story that's too small. The paradox is that if life is "all about me," then life doesn't have all that much meaning. But if I'm part of a grand story with meaning and purpose, no matter how small my role is, my life shares in that meaning and purpose.

Like much of reality, the challenge is to give each thing its due and to hold opposites in balance. On the one hand, as Bogie said to Bergman in *Casablanca,* our little worries "don't amount to a hill of beans." On the other hand, we are beloved of God, made in the image and likeness of God, and worthy enough that God's Son died for us on the cross. We get into trouble when we stress one of these truths to the exclusion of the other.

HOW A TOO-SMALL STORY LIMITS OUR CHILDREN

Being told they are good gives our children a sense of power. Tying their story in to a larger story tells them what the power's for.

We have to make sure our children get the whole story. We can help our children find their true identity—and we can fire their imagination—by letting them know they are part of a magnificent story: We come from God and through our lives have the opportunity to truly better the world by bringing God's kingdom to life in the here and now. And ultimately we have a destiny of happiness beyond our current ability to imagine.

When I look at the world we present to kids in popular media, I cringe. The worst of it is not the sex or the violence or the self-centeredness per se. The worst of it is the empti-ness of the life we hold out to them. Those who have tried it will tell you that rampant sexual promiscuity leaves you empty and totally alone. A life of brutalizing others is brutal. Being the center of your own universe makes for a petty and cramped life. "Is that all I'm worth?" our kids are asking us. At their baptism we spoke for them: "Do you reject Satan and all his empty promises?" If these media depictions aren't empty promises, I don't know what they are.

True sexual expression is good and wonderful. Power and authority used well are admirable. Having a positive sense of self is healthy and good. But though modern culture pretends to be selling these positive traits, it's delivering something quite different.

We need to counter the shabby and empty promises of modern culture with a truth we've come to know in our own hearts and lives. We can find that truth by opening our hearts and lives to the message of the gospel.

Compare a few of the messages your kids hear on TV and other media with Jesus' message.

MEDIA	JESUS
You deserve a break today.	Take up your cross and follow me.
Have sex anytime, anywhere, with anyone.	Neither do I condemn you; go and sin no more.
Satisfy every appetite as soon as possible.	Not by bread alone do you live.
Look out for number one.	Seek first the kingdom of God.
Appearance is everything.	Blessed are the pure in heart.
If you're angry, it's OK to be violent.	Turn the other cheek.
Odd people don't belong.	Whoever does the will of my Father is my brother and sister and mother.
Don't acknowledge that a quarter of the world is starving tonight.	Whatever you do to the least of these, you do to me.

HOW TO CONNECT OUR CHILDREN'S STORIES TO THE LARGER STORY

We can learn a lot from the success of gangs. Look at the appeal of gangs: How do they attract such loyalty and commitment? How do they get kids to risk their lives for the group? Gangs provide lost and lonely kids with a feeling of belonging to a group with a purpose and an important, exciting story.

Gangs have emblems (often Christian symbols). Do you have any Christian art or symbols in your home? Gangs have heroes. Do your kids know about the heroic lives of the saints? (Be sure to get resources that present full-dimensional portraits of the saints, not the goody-two-shoes versions that are often offered.) Gangs require sacrifice. Do you give your kids a chance to put out effort for the practice of their faith, for the community, or for the common good in the world? Gangs have special signs of greeting. Do you bless your children when they come and go? Do you begin family meals with prayer? Gangs tie you in to a whole group of people. Do you celebrate or get together with extended family and family friends? Gangs are built around loyalty. Do your kids know that they matter to you? that you would die for them? Or do other pursuits and interests come before them?

Taking action **20**

How to link your children to others' stories

Tell your children about your favorite saint, your favorite apostle, your favorite stories from the Old and New Testaments.

Introduce your children to Bible stories. Some great ones in the Old Testament: Adam and Eve, Cain and Abel, Noah, Samson.

Put the manger scene out early every Christmas. Church historians say that St. Francis taught all of Europe about the theory of the Incarnation by popularizing the display of the manger scene in every town and village.

Cut down on the mental junk food, and give your family something morally nutritious. Fill your house with good books, videos, and movies. Limit the number of empty stories your children experience, like those that value things over people, comfort and ease above virtue and courage. Read good books aloud to your children. When our daughters were younger (and even today when our hectic lives land us all in the same place for a spell), Kathleen would read aloud to the whole family. Often this would be on cold winter nights, and we'd each find a cozy place to sprawl out. In candlelight, she'd read of the adventures of Laura Ingalls and her family on the prairie. She would read books about courage and honor, generosity and passion. A friend recommends *The Watsons Go to Birmingham—1963,* in which a black family from Flint, Michigan, travels to Alabama during troubled times. She says it's a touching and funny story offering a very real portrayal of family life and sibling relations and also a great portrayal of the power of the extended family.

Encourage your children's creativity so that they will be less swayed by stories with simplistic answers to complex problems. Notice how one-dimensional characters are repeatedly force-fed to children by Disney, McDonald's, TV networks, and so on. If you limit your children's imagination, you cripple their ability to grow spiritually in the future.

Encourage

your children to create their own stories, plays, and characters, or buy them uplifting books on tape so they can employ their imagination as they listen.

Help

your children meet other people, especially from other cultures and ethnic groups, who hold the same values you do, whether at church, at work, in community organizations, or in the neighborhood.

Help

your children find ways to be involved as a contributing member of their community.

Bring

your family to another church in your synod or region or, for Catholics, to your diocese's cathedral for Mass and a tour some Sunday. Often someone there will be glad to give you a tour and explain some of the church's history. Help your children realize that their faith is a universal one.

Make sure you tell your children about Catholic Charities and how much good this agency does. As an archbishop of Canterbury once wrote, "The Church is the only society that exists for the benefit of people who are not its members." Check this out. Help your children tune in to the many good things that people of faith are doing in the world. Help them see how they are part of that effort.

Get mailings from Catholic Relief Services, and support a religious missionary order to get information about the work its members do around the world. This global story transcends space and time.

Explain the Campaign for Human Development and the good work it does, and explain that we have a Peter's Pence collection to support the universal church, which serves people around the world.

At the end of his life, Albert Einstein had one final question. He understood the physical principles of the universe better than anyone else of his time and up until his time. But still the question remained for him: "Is the universe friendly?" I take that to mean, "Is there a place for me here?" The only way to answer such questions is with a story. We tell stories to find our place in the world. Without such a story, with only the bare scientific facts—though undeniably magnificent in themselves—we bang up against the question that Einstein had in his waning days. And we also have the central question of all existence: "Why am I here?"

The response we find in Genesis is that God looked out over the formless void and, seeing only chaos, poured forth light and order and life to the whole universe, creating it out of God's own self. The answer we have from Jesus in the New Testament is that in the beginning was the Word, that is, meaning and sense and God's self-expression. In the beginning was communication. A word spoken into a void longs to connect with "the other." We were created to be "the other" to whom God speaks. God has a story to tell. Don't let your children go through life unaware that they have a leading role to play in that story.

A Closer Look

Darryl's Story

I remember seeing a headline on an article in *The New Yorker* that asked, "Do Parents Matter?" The article argued that in the modern age parents really don't matter that much in the development of children. As I read the argument, fierce pain formed in my chest. I'll tell you why.

Years ago I worked at a child-care facility outside Chicago. The kids there were wards of the state. Some were orphans, but most were from families that were having such troubles that they were unable to care for these children—at least for the time being. The institution I worked for took them in and cared for them. Most of the kids suffered deep emotional pain as a result of the separation from their families.

I was the activities counselor for the five- to nine-year-olds. I had also spent the summer at camp with them, and we had grown very close. When Thanksgiving came, most of the boys were going to celebrate the day with relatives. Those who didn't have a place to go were going to join me at my mother's table, where she had generously invited us all to partake of a Thanksgiving feast.

As I gathered up the guys who were going to join me, I noticed Darryl and his brother, Steven, sitting anxiously by the hall's entrance door. They were dressed in their finest, all scrubbed and handsome. They were waiting for their mother to pick them up as she had promised to do. They were getting antsy. I hated to leave them, but time and turkey wait for no man. I gave the two boys each a friendly slug on the shoulder and led my dinner companions out into the cold November air.

Later that night I returned with my gang of celebrators. We were a boisterous crowd coming up the stairs to the residence hall. When we burst through the doorway, I was greeted by a horrendous punch, full force into my solar plexus. I was shocked and winded. I could barely mutter one word: "Darryl?"

His eyes smoldered, and I thought he was going to give me another blast. But instead he blurted out, "She never came!" He stared at me with rage. Then he did something I'd never seen him do before. He cried. He pounded my shoulders, and he cried. I tried to hold him, but he would not be contained. He cried out his fury to the heavens, and I had no words to say.

That jolt of pain I felt as Darryl lashed out is what I felt again when I saw the headline arguing that parents don't make a difference. Tell that to Darryl.

Later that night, when all the kids had finally settled down, prayers had been said, the bedtime story had been told, and all the boys had drifted off to sleep, I talked with Sister Gertrude, who was in charge of that hall and the primary caretaker for these sixteen boys. She said she'd seen a pattern with Darryl's relatives. It may have been drugs, or it may have been alcohol. It may have been immaturity, shame, or plain selfishness. But the pattern was one of promises made and promises broken.

Sister Gertrude had come to face the annual approach of the holidays with a certain amount of trepidation. All the kids would tend to act up some, but certain kids would reexperience early wounds, and all the pain would return full force. Being handy and safe, she often caught the brunt of it.

Parents don't matter? Tell that to the kid waiting for the mother who never shows. Tell that to the kid whose father never once said a positive thing to him. Tell that to the child whose uncle abused her and whose parents wouldn't acknowledge it.

We're not just launching pads from which our children float away and never connect. We are connected, and what we do matters. I was always amazed at how much their parents meant to these kids, especially those who had been treated so badly by their parents. "Someday my dad's gonna buy me a ten-speed bike," one would say. "Yeah, man, well, my dad said he's gonna buy me a dirt bike when I'm sixteen."

These parents had power. And many of them had good intentions. What they didn't have was maturity of character. That, or their character was diminished by addiction to alcohol or drugs. In all cases, what was missing was consistent follow-through. Consistency is essential in preparing children for faith. We try to tell them about the promises of God. Who would believe these promises if they never experienced them in normal life?

In many of the success stories, where parents found the strength and wherewithal to get their act together and become responsible, caring parents, it was love for their children that propelled them to change. Surely not all of them made it. Who can judge them? Not I. But I know that their children were on their side, rooting for their success and offering them the chance to get outside of their selfish worldview and love another person more than their own immediate concerns. After all, that is the most transforming power in the world. The love between a parent and a child—that certainly matters!

You have the tools to
build the kingdom of God.
Pass them on well worn.

A BUMPER STICKER FROM

THE SECULAR FRANCISCANS

CHAPTER FOURTEEN

Thirst for Justice
Making the System Work for Everybody

I have a hunch that many people's worldview changed the day astronauts aboard *Apollo 8* sent back a crisp, clear photo of the earth as seen from outer space. I remember looking at that photo of a planet, a planet I happened to live on, and feeling as though I were seeing it for the first time. The photo was taken on Christmas Eve of 1968.

Here was this "big blue marble," looking serene and majestic, tracing its way along its appointed orbit, hung like a precious ornament in the vastness of space. I meditated on that image for a while, and it dawned on me that this pristine-looking globe was teeming with life, life that was astoundingly various and abundant and interconnected.

From space you can see no borderlines between countries—even warring countries. From space you cannot see where the U.S. leaves off and Mexico begins. You cannot see a line of demarcation between Northern Ireland and the Republic of Ireland, between Israel and Lebanon, between Serbia and Kosovo, between China and Tibet, between Ecuador and Peru.

What you can see—and it can be both wondrous and frightening to contemplate—is a single planet upon whose well-being all its resident species rely. Our fate is one, interconnected, and utterly fragile. On that Christmas Eve of 1968, after a bloody century bespoiled by the unholy lust of nationalism, Earth's inhabitants were presented a new image to live by.

What a different frontier from what greeted the first European settlers to come to North America. Faced with seemingly endless land and possibilities, pioneers could afford to believe that they could chart their own course as rugged individualists. What a man did on his own conquered land was nobody else's business. What the other man did on his land (few women owned or controlled land) was nobody's business either. Just "don't tread on me."

These rules applied selectively to only those who were "like me"—those whose skin was the same color and whose culture resembled my own. Which left Europeans, who were militarily advanced compared to other peoples, free to exert their will over the lives of others who were seen as less than fully human. With such a mind-set, it made sense for aggressive nations to carve up the world into their own possessions and to assume the blessing of God on all this overpowering, carving, and adventuring. Such conquest of whole peoples was seen as a good thing, a way to bring order to this messy world. Though challenged in the ensuing decades, remnants of this view hold current yet today.

SPACESHIP EARTH WITHOUT A PADDLE

But then, literally out of the blue, we got a different perspective, a different view of our world and our place on it. Rather than seeing the world as chaos to be tamed, we saw the earth, with its beauty and majesty, as a shining opal in a whole new setting. The planet grew in importance, and our place as humans shifted. From a high position of independent agent mastering his environment, we suddenly slid down the scale to a mere life-form among many seeking ways to at least survive and, we hoped, to thrive.

This new view has sunk into our subconscious, where it slowly alters our thinking. Will it catch on? The evidence is not encouraging. The hopeful view is that more and more people will perceive that we are more than individuals battling for our own piece of the planet. We are all in this together. As residents of Spaceship Earth, we share a common fate. Yet our world is rife with turf conflict, neighbor battling neighbor and apparently willing to destroy all rather than consider compromise as equals.

It's no longer true—and we've learned the hard way that it was never true—that what I do on my property matters not to others. We've got toxic-waste sites that will take billions of dollars to clean up. We've got a hole in the ozone layer that seems to be expanding. We've got a history of slavery and colonialism that has totally wiped out certain cultures and severely damaged whole peoples, with effects cascading down multiple generations.

Yet we're all in the same boat.

Maybe that's one of the reasons the movie *Titanic* was so popular. Not to take away from the world-class special effects, the heart-tugging love story featuring a popular teen heartthrob, and that ubiquitous hit theme song, but I think the plot hit on a theme that resonated deeply with society's common, underlying fears. The Titanic was huge, new, and powerful. It was cruising along, serenely impervious to any dangers.

That's been the image of our economy during the last years of the twentieth century. It's huge and powerful, and it seems to be cruising along, impervious to any dangers. Our way of life is touted as being indestructible. But lurking in the shadows of our subconscious is the fear that a virtual iceberg is looming in the gathering darkness, and it's got our name on it.

Many books for parents concentrate on the small world of the home and school. But what kind of a world are we preparing our children to live in? Can we prepare them for the challenges they will face? What skills must they acquire in order to live out their faith in the realities of this world?

Family life, well lived, presents a paradigm for social justice. "The family ideally is the institution that claims to be committed to all of its members *for better or for worse*," said Victoria Lee Erickson. "The family is the oldest institution, even older than religion itself." The family is the first place in all of human history, as well as in each of our lives, where we learn the rules of fairness, compensation, compromise, trust, loyalty, and order.

It's interesting that social justice, which aims to create a system that works for everyone and promotes harmony, peace, and unity, is looked upon with such dread by most people. Even religious people committed to applying their faith in every other aspect of life can shy away from social-justice work. It's scary. It involves confrontation and possibly conflict. It is going to upset whatever equilibrium we have managed to scrape together in this world of rapid change. Too often, social action is reduced to a caricature of itself: the ornery, strident, adversarial person who is never satisfied and always stirring up trouble. Conflict and confrontation will certainly be a part of social change at any level—family, neighborhood, state, or world. But unity, cooperation, friendship, and care are also part of that picture. And global change is more than most people can wrap their mind around.

WHOSE FAMILY VALUES?

From our earliest days, when it begins with just "me and Mommy," our task in maturing spiritually is to expand our sense of connection to others in the world. We are always re-evaluating our answer to the question "Who is my neighbor?" Jesus answered that question with a story we've come to know as the parable of the good Samaritan.

> A man was going down from Jerusalem to Jericho, and fell into the hands of robbers, who stripped him, beat him, and went away, leaving him half dead. Now by chance a priest was going down that road; and when he saw him, he passed by on the other side. So likewise a Levite, when he came to the place and saw him, passed by on the other side. But a Samaritan while traveling came near him; and when he saw him, he was moved with pity. He went to him and bandaged his wounds, having poured oil and wine on them. Then he put him on his own animal, brought him to an inn, and took care of him. The next day he took out two denarii, gave them to the innkeeper, and said, "Take care of him; and when I come back, I will repay you whatever more you spend." Which of these three, do you think, was a neighbor to the man who fell into the hands of the robbers? (Luke 10:30–36)

Many people talk about family values. The family values that Jesus espoused for the human family are captured in this and other parables. Robert Ellsberg, writing in *The Living Pulpit*, highlighted three values that Jesus held up that can be seen as family values.

The first value is inclusiveness rather than exclusiveness

Jesus did not limit his attention to his immediate family or even to the acceptable people in society. Throughout his career he was attended by scandal because of the "family" he gathered around him: prostitutes and other immoral people, despised tax collectors, unclean people. "The 'family' that Jesus gathers around him is hardly what we would call an 'exclusive club,'" wrote Ellsberg. "Instead it includes every type of 'wrong' person . . . excluded by the prevailing standards of social value."

The second value is humility as opposed to power

Ellsberg identified humility as a family value exemplified by Jesus' life. "The new family of Jesus should not reflect the values of a society in which the powerful lord it over the powerless. Rather, in this family whoever would be first must become 'the last of all and the servant of all.'" Jesus was not concerned with overturning authority, but to put authority's purpose in proper context. He asked the a priori question "What's the power for?" In his hierarchy of values, power and authority are to be used for the good of all, the body of Christ.

The third value is discipleship versus kinship

Discipleship was and is a radical message. The world of Jesus' day was organized around families and clans. To the clan you owed everything; to the outsider, nothing. Jesus turned this principle upside down. He redefined what family means. When his mother and other family members were worried for his well-being and came to take him home, he responded, "Whoever does the will of God is my brother and sister and mother." That leaves it open to everyone in the world.

Social justice is impossible without an experience of solidarity, the knowledge that those who seem to be strangers are indeed my brothers and sisters. Family life can either close our children into a life of small concerns or equip them with the tools they'll need in order to work for and establish justice in their neighborhoods and communities—even the global community. This is a tall order. But as with the rest of life, it begins quite simply and locally. It begins in the home with the development of empathy, justice, and solidarity.

BEGIN WITH EMPATHY

In his landmark book *The Moral Child: Nurturing Children's Natural Moral Growth,* William Damon told the story of a two-year-old who, seeing another toddler crying, brought his mother over to soothe the sad child. Even though the crying child's mother was at hand, the compassionate kid wanted to offer a surefire remedy: his own mommy. This child may have had to work on the details, but he was well on his way to developing a fine moral sense.

Empathy is the fundamental building block of the moral life. Jesus told the Pharisees that all of biblical morality can be captured in the saying "Love God with your whole heart, mind, and soul, and your neighbor as yourself." There's no living out the second half of that commandment without a sense of connectedness to and empathy for others. Don't hit. Don't steal. Why not? Possibly the first verbal moral lesson children receive is the gently posed question "Well, how would you like it if that were done to you?"

The key to navigating such basic low-level moral issues is a sense of compassion. And compassion means identifying, at least remotely, with those who would be hurt by our actions. It's only after mastering the fundamentals of empathy and compassion that our children will one day be able to master the more complex and difficult moral and ethical questions that will face them—questions about genetic engineering, global economic justice, and just what constitutes a legitimate deduction on their income-tax returns.

But be careful. "How would *you* like it?" is a question that can be thrown in our kids' faces like a slap. Instead, use the question as an invitation to self-understanding and growth as a moral person in the world. If you make room for your child's array of feelings (from the selfish to the selfless, the venal to the gloriously giving), your child will, over time, develop the capacity to imagine the plight and feelings of others with care and compassion.

Taking action 21

How to foster empathy

in your kids

Make it a clear expectation, from early on, that sharing is a part of living in a family as well as living in society. It may be tempting to try to avoid the minor conflicts that kids get into over whose turn it is to use a piece of sports equipment, a toy, or a bike. But this is valuable practice for later in life. When I was a camp counselor, I faced the problem of having sixteen kids of various skill levels scheduled to enjoy the trampoline. The kids always complained that they didn't get enough time. I invited the boys from B Cabin to come up with their own rules for how they would divvy up their sixty minutes each week on the trampoline. We wouldn't begin the activity until they were all content with the plan. Though this preparation exercise had its challenges, it was possibly the most productive way to build a sense of fairness and mutual caring among the boys.

Ask your kids to imagine themselves living as one of the characters in a book they're reading or a TV show they're watching. Say, "What would you do if you were there?"

Stop your kids when you see them acting cruel or unkind, and review the situation together. It's easy for kids to be cruel to one another. They need our help to correct their "vision." They can act cruelly only if they don't see that we are all one and that when one part of the body of Christ is hurting, we all hurt.

Open your home and your world to a variety of people. Associate with people of other cultures and ethnic backgrounds. Don't make this a case of tokenism; build honest relationships based on mutual interest and trust.

Encourage

your kids to read biographies of the saints. I remember my dad coming home from a retreat bearing copies of *Damien the Leper* for us kids to read. I've still got my copy on my bookshelf at work. Here was a heroic story about a man who demonstrated the ultimate in compassion.

Talk

about situations from your daily life that illustrate your own sense of empathy and compassion. Kids are all ears when you talk about the real stories of what goes on at work, in the neighborhood, or in the extended family.

Review

situations at your kids' school that call for compassion. Talk about those times when a new kid arrives and feels lonely, when a kid loses his lunch in front of the whole class, when someone struggles with a school subject or is different from the other kids. Ask aloud, "I wonder what life is like for that kid right now?"

Recite

the Prayer of St. Francis ("Lord, make me an instrument of your peace . . .") regularly at meals or bedtime. This prayer captures the essence of compassionate living. Give a copy of the prayer to your kids.

AFTER EMPATHY, JUSTICE

After you foster empathy in your children, their identification with others will help them see what society is so good at ignoring—the inherent unfairness in the system. When we're divorced from other people's lives and realities, we cannot know their circumstances. Such distance leads to heartless comments and horrible social policy. When told the peasants had no bread, Marie Antoinette said, "Then let them eat cake." We have to teach our kids to identify with others so that they might see reality from the vantage point of those who are suffering.

In an introduction to Michael True's book *Homemade Social Justice,* columnist Sidney Callahan talked about how families can help children learn to see the subtleties of social injustice.

> Violence and oppression can be so embedded and hidden in a social system that a special education of the eye and heart is needed for proper perception and perspective. Families are where we learn to see and feel. Only our life together produces the possibility of peace and justice, so we can start here, and now. With hope.

Is such blindness overstated? Author Kevin Axe told a story about the kind of blindness that can occur in otherwise perceptive people. He and his wife belonged to a book club/faith-sharing group. They were discussing a book about relations between racial groups in the workplace. One of the participants, whose husband was a top executive in a local company, remarked in all sincerity, "Well, we really wouldn't have much to say on that topic. They don't hire any of *them* where Joe works."

259

It's hard to solve a problem you don't know you're creating. As Sister Kathleen Hughes, R.S.C.J., said, "Reconciliation cannot happen in a community where the majority believe that they don't need it and the minority don't deserve it."

That special education of the eye and heart is a crucial part of your child's moral formation.

Catholic social teaching underscores both the dignity of the individual and the value of the community. We have to teach our kids to live with the tension of keeping those "goods" in balance. The goal we aspire to is solidarity, where individuals choose to stand with one another for the common good.

Taking action 22

How to educate your children
about justice

Educate yourself. Read newspapers and listen to talk radio when people from other cultures call in. Don't just read what you already know and agree with. It's good to hear another perspective.

Share stories of injustice from our history. This should not become a shame-and-blame operation. Rather, the point is that we need to acknowledge that unfairness can be subtle and embedded in systems that appear morally good. It's part of any complete moral education.

Explain to your children that social systems are a mixed bag containing policies and practices that can produce both good and bad results. For example, city government can give tax breaks to land developers who will build housing and parkland that beautifies a blighted area. And while many people benefit, some of those citizens who are the least able to fend for themselves are evicted and left without a place to go. In his book *Homemade Social Justice* Michael True quoted a woman: "The problem is not to shield children from injustice and violence (because you can't anyway), but to make them thoughtful about such things."

Help your children see through the smoke screens. For example, when slavery was being challenged, many slave owners responded with stories of how well they treated their slaves, never even seeing the basic question of what right a person could have to *own* another person. The same was true with the question of women's right to vote. Much talk centered on how many social privileges women had rather than whether a society can be run with half of its members unable to participate in its governance.

The glory of the American experiment is the high value we place on freedom. Its shadow side is the inordinately high value we can place on individualism. Freedom to speak, assemble, worship, and pursue happiness has been a blessing to the world. The rise of individualism at the expense of the family and other communities has left disruption in its wake.

COME AND GET IT!

The best school for solidarity is the Eucharist. My late friend Ann Graff used to sum up her vision of the church in the world with this phrase: "Everybody eats!" No one is excluded from the table; no one goes away hungry. That attitude surely sums up Jesus' public ministry. When Jesus ate, no one was turned away.

We may come to the table of the Eucharist as fragmented selves and fragmented communities. But through faith we can begin to see not fragmentation but wholeness. A while back, one of our parish priests, Father Bob Bolser, C.S.V., began the 10 A.M. Mass with an opening reflection: "Seeing is believing, some folks say. But it could also be said that believing is seeing."

He told a story to illustrate his point. His father was born blind. For years and years young Bob Bolser prayed that his father would receive a miracle, that he would be allowed to see. "For even the briefest of moments I wanted with all my heart for him to see my face and know what I looked like," Bolser told the congregation gathered that Sunday morning.

All the family prayed. Bob's brother, a pilot in the air force, even visited Lourdes and sent home a quart of water from that shrine, but their father remained blind.

> It was years later, after novenas and rosaries and prayers and promises, that I finally came to a new realization. Our prayers for my father had been answered a thousand times over. All these years I had longed for him to see what I looked like, and all the while he had always known who I was. I wanted him to see my face; rather, he'd forever known my heart.

After the homily, most of the congregation gathered around the altar. We sang out heartily during the eucharistic prayer. We held hands at the Our Father and greeted one another warmly at the sign of peace. As the people—young and old, liberal and conservative, healthy and sick, of various nationalities and ethnic groups—streamed up for communion I realized that during the Mass our vision had indeed improved.

We may have walked into church thinking we were all separate individuals, on our own in this world. Now we were held together with the knowledge that we were one body, a holy people, gathered together by Christ. Father Bob called forth our belief, and we saw with new eyes.

Catholicism in the U.S. encompasses some of the wealthiest and most powerful citizens as well as some of the poorest immigrants struggling to survive. They may end up in the same church on Sunday. Claretian father Rosendo Urabazzo spoke of what he sees when he celebrates Mass in his Texas parish. "They enter and sit where they may. The haves and the have-nots sit side by side on the same bench. In God's eyes we are all equal as human beings. Would that it would be that way outside of church."

The Eucharist can give us vision, and vision can fire our imagination to create in the world the unity we celebrate and sometimes experience at worship. The Eucharist is the bread for our journey, giving us strength for the hard work of building the kingdom of justice and mercy. The Eucharist transforms us, healing those weaknesses that keep us from justice, fairness, generosity, and peace.

The beatitude reads, "Blessed are those who hunger and thirst for justice." It takes a true hunger and thirst in order to do the hard work necessary to achieve justice. You can't just have a mild hankering for it. You'll be frustrated and thwarted and distracted all too easily.

Taking **23** action

How to teach your children solidarity

Expose your children to different types of liturgies, such as an urban Way of the Cross. This liturgy can help them make the connection between Christ's passion at the hands of violent oppressors and the fate suffered by many people today. The 8th Day Center in Chicago hosts an annual Good Friday march that visits a place in the city—like the Cook County Jail—that corresponds to the passion that Jesus suffered.

Work for a political candidate who shares your values of inclusion and equal opportunity. Involve your children to the extent that age allows. If you want to affect public policies and laws, politics is how such things get done. We have a moral obligation to know how our laws and policies are affecting the poor and defenseless, the least among us.

Tie experiences of consumerism to an awareness of others. The biggest threat to your children's sense of solidarity in our culture is the lure of easy living, excess, and comfort. You can counteract that attraction. My third-grade teacher, Miss Betty Schmidt, was an amazing spiritual influence on all her students. When pressed on it one day, she explained that whatever she spent on entertainment or luxuries for herself, she gave an equal amount to the poor. This was over and above what she gave to the church. All on a Catholic schoolteacher's salary!

Kevin Axe had a similar idea with a holiday twist. Feeling squeamish over how much was spent at Christmas one year, he decided that the following year he'd buy his Christmas presents twice. He'd buy a reasonable amount for the family and arrange to give the same amount in cash or gifts to people in need. This spiritual exercise can be a great awareness builder—both of how much your family spends on luxuries and of how much need there is in the world.

Another take on this idea comes from Father John Kavanaugh, S.J., who suggested ways to balance solidarity with consumerism. He suggested, "For every shopping excursion, you should have an excursion into relationships. If you go shopping one time, then you should spend some time playing with your kids or going for a walk with your spouse or sitting down and giving thanks for the gifts of life."

Don't go it alone.

Lone rangers don't last long working to create justice in the world. Michael True, author of *Homemade Social Justice*, wrote, "The company one keeps provides a life-saving support system."

You will play a major role in fostering a hunger for justice in your children. You will be the one who teaches them how to handle conflicts, and you will model how it's done. You're going to train them in the ways of negotiating and settling disputes with others in the home. The question is, What principles underlie your teaching? Is it "Get the best deal no matter how much you screw the other guy"? Is it

> *If you want peace, work for justice.*
>
> Pope Paul VI

"Truth is relative, and you use as much or as little of it as you need to get out of a jam"? Or do you know and encourage the principles of Catholic social and moral teaching?

This task is not easy to do on your own, but there are many resources available to help. See the lists in the back of this book.

The responsibility can seem overwhelming, but you don't have to solve all the world's problems, nor can you expect your children to. The point is to be part of the solution rather than part of the problem. Alone, this is impossible, with God and God's other partners here on earth, anything is possible. As Father Daniel Berrigan, S.J., told the editors of *U.S. Catholic,* "No one, even with the most fervent of wills, can do everything. But the moral distance between doing something and doing nothing is momentous indeed."

Prayer for Peace and Justice in My Child's Lifetime

Time to update the will, said Bob the lawyer.
The kids will be taken care of, have a shot at
    starting life
if "anything should happen."
Any other gifts or causes to support?

Why not the homeless shelter that our parish
    serves? I thought.
Profound sadness rolled in like a winter fog,
not unexpected when making out a will.
But I don't plan to die soon.
And I've come to accept my very real limitations.
But when I was young and full of heart,
I never thought my days would pass,
and still men would sleep on shaky cots in
    basement halls,
sweltering in the summer, bone chilled in the
    winter.
Oh, children, forgive me
for this legacy.
Chili pots on a Wednesday night,
third Wednesday of every month.

It is good to have an end to journey toward, but it is the journey that matters, in the end.

URSULA K. LEGUIN

CHAPTER FIFTEEN

You're Doing Fine, and Help Is on the Way

Did you hear about the guy who went off to college and was surprised to discover that all these years he'd been writing prose and never realized it? Well, all these years—whether you knew it or not—you've been walking a spiritual path. And the moments you've spent being a parent are part of that path.

One of my favorite authors, Dolores Curran, interviewed Sister Mary Luke Tobin, a remarkable woman who's had great influence on church reform during the twentieth century. Luke, as she is widely known, had just turned ninety when Curran thought it would be a good idea to capture some of her wisdom. Curran asked, "Have you ever had a mystical experience? If so, could you share it with us?"

Luke replied, "That's an easy one. Yes. All of life is a mystical experience."

May we all enjoy such twenty-twenty vision! If all of life is a mystical experience (and I believe it is), then every moment you spend as a parent is a mystical experience. You are on a mystical journey from the first moment of excitement at the birth of your child through every dark valley and golden mountaintop and all the meandering roads along the way.

As you cultivate that vision of family life as your spiritual path, take comfort that you are not alone when you face new challenges each day.

A final story captures what I mean. A friend of mine, Sister Sheryl Chen, O.C.S.O., is a cloistered nun. She told me this story, a kind of parable, and it gives me great comfort in my role as father. Sister Sheryl was living at Santa Rita Abbey in the high desert of southern Arizona, near the Mexican border. The nuns' days began early, with 3 A.M. prayer. One December morning just before prayer was to begin, Sister Sheryl stepped out into the crisp night air to do one of her chores. In the stillness of the cold, clear, Advent night, she cast her gaze into the diamond sky. One bright star among thousands caught her eye, and she wondered, "How is it that a lowly nun, by chance wandering this desert hillside on an early December morn, is met by the light of this distant star?"

Being one of the brightest people I know, Sheryl began to calculate the vast distance of that star and how long it would take its light to reach that very spot of hillside where she stood, her face awash in starlight. And being one of the holiest people I know, Sheryl began to reflect on how much like God's love that starlight was: traveling through space and time to greet her that Advent morning, right there, right then.

The same is true for you. Perhaps you feel uncertain as a parent. When you look to the future, you may be filled with doubts and fears. But you can have faith that even now, God's love is on its way to meet you in those moments you fear. That is the message of Advent: light overcoming the darkness, love overcoming fear.

So let us go forward, walking in the expectation of starlight, certain that God's love is with us and our children now and is winging its way to us forever. Amen.

Selected Resources

Here is a list of books that I drew from in developing my thinking on family life as a spiritual path. These books share a sense that being a parent is a spiritual adventure wherein to discover the wonders of your children, yourself, and your God. T.M.

Also, Cathy O'Connell-Cahill and I produce *At Home with Our Faith,* a newsletter to nurture the spirituality of families. For more information on this monthly newsletter, call 1-800-328-6515 or go to www.homefaith.com.

Berends, Polly Berrien. *Whole Child / Whole Parent.* New York: Harper & Row, 1983.

Berends, Polly Berrien. *Gently Lead: How to Teach Your Children about God While Finding Out for Yourself.* New York: Harper Collins, 1991.

Coloroso, Barbara. *Kids Are Worth It! Giving Your Child the Gift of Inner Discipline.* New York: Avon Books, 1994.

Covey, Stephen R. *The Seven Habits of Highly Effective Families.* New York: Golden Books, 1997.

Curran, Dolores. *Traits of a Healthy Family.* Minneapolis, Minn.: Winston Press, 1983.

Curran, Dolores. *Tired of Arguing With Your Kids? Wisdom from Parents Who Have Been There.* Notre Dame, Ind.: Sorin Books, 1999.

Gurian, Michael. *A Fine Young Man.* New York: Tarcher/ Putnam, 1998.

Johnson, Anne, and Vic Goodman. *The Essence of Parenting: Becoming the Parent You Want to Be.* New York: Crossroad, 1995.

O'Connell-Chesto, Kathleen. *Raising Kids Who Care: About Themselves, about Their World, about Each Other.* Franklin, Wis.: Sheed & Ward, 1997.

O'Connell-Chesto, Kathleen. *Why are the Dandelions Weeds?* Liguori, Mo.: Liguori, 1999.

Pipher, Mary, Ph.D. *Reviving Ophelia: Saving the Selves of Adolescent Girls.* New York: Ballantine Books, 1994.

Pollack, William, Ph.D. *Real Boys.* New York: Owl Books, 1998.

Sasso, Steve, and Pat Sasso. *10 Best Gifts for Your Teen: Raising Teens with Love and Understanding.* Notre Dame, Ind.: Sorin Books, 1999.

Taffel, Ron, M.D., and Melinda Blau. *Nurturing Good Children Now.* New York: Golden Books, 1999.

Wright, Wendy M. *Sacred Dwelling: A Spirituality of Family Life.* New York: Crossroad, 1989.

Wuthnow, Robert. *Growing Up Religious: Christians and Jews and Their Journeys of Faith.* Boston: Beacon Press, 1999.